They Made You the Boss, Now What?

A Practical Guide for New Leaders

D1571222

Les Duncan

PublishAmerica
Baltimore

First printing

ISBN: 1-4137-3182-1
PUBLISHED BY PUBLISHAMERICA, LLLP
www.publishamerica.com
Baltimore

Printed in the United States of America

To My Wife Sharon,
My Lover, My Best Friend and
The Greatest Thing That Ever Happened to Me.

I Thank God Every Day that She is a Part of My Life.

Every Day I Pray

That Everyone I Meet Will Experience God's Love In All That I Say and In All That I Do.

And

That Everyone I Meet Will Be Better Off, No Matter How Brief Our Encounter.

Many thanks to the following people for helping me with this book:
Jason Capitel
Sharon Duncan
Michael Flaherty
David Haak
Andy Laudato
Farren Mervicker
Nicole Michael
Bonnie McElearney
Paul Watkins

Table of Contents

Foreword

It was Wednesday, September 11, 2002 – the one year anniversary for the Al Qaeda terrorist attacks on our country. I woke up excited that most television and radio networks were devoting virtually their entire programming day to tributes of this tragic event. I had my TiVo programmed to tape many of the shows while I was working and my wife and I planned to watch them over the next few evenings at home.

I rose early – as I usually do. I didn't feel well. I had a headache that had been getting progressively worse for several days and I felt a bit spacey. I told myself that I had just been working too hard. It had been a busy year and I really needed a vacation.

A friend of mine had invited me to play golf at an exclusive golf club the next day, and I *had* to clear my calendar at work before I could do this. I told myself that I *had* to go to work on September 11, 2002 because I really wanted to be off playing golf the next day. In addition, we had a special 9/11 tribute planned at work that I didn't want to miss.

I made my way to the office but only lasted half a day. I spent the remainder of the day at home, resting. I went to bed that evening expecting to feel better the next day. I had visited the doctor for a routine check up just a week before, and everything had been OK.

I knew the symptoms, and although I was experiencing some of them, they were not nearly as bad as those I had experienced when my brain bled a few years earlier. During that episode, I was unable to stand up. I crawled back and forth from my bed to the bathroom because I couldn't walk. My wife had to help dress me. I ended up having brain surgery and the doctors removed a faulty blood vessel. It took me months to recover and get back to work. Certainly whatever was happening to me now was not the same thing. Nothing to worry about, I told myself. There would be *no* more surgery performed on my brain.

The next day was Thursday, September 12, 2002. I awoke. I was grateful for that, just as I had been grateful for each and every day since my first brain hemorrhage. It is true that serious health problems can completely change your attitude toward and your perspective on life.

I was fixing breakfast, when I suddenly felt much worse. The vision in my left eye was a little blurry. My left ear ached and my hearing was slightly impaired. My head hurt even worse – the pain was almost unbearable. The left side of my face began to feel numb and I had a light tingling sensation in my left leg.

I knew that there would be no golf with my friend at a prestigious golf club that day. I also knew that I wouldn't be watching tributes to 9/11 with my wife any time soon.

I called to my wife and simply said, "I think you had better take me to the emergency room – I am pretty sure I am having another brain hemorrhage."

At the emergency room they take brain hemorrhages seriously. I was whisked away immediately – ahead of many others who have been waiting to be seen with less serious ailments. They put me in a room and hooked me up to heart, pulse, blood pressure and other vital sign monitors, and they stuck an oxygen hose in my nostrils. Minutes later I was wheeled away for a CAT scan. No one said anything, but I could tell from the whispering and grim faces that something was very wrong. I went directly from a CAT scan to a MRI.

Just minutes later I was back in my room hooked up to all the same monitors and the ER doctor came to tell me what I already knew – my brain was bleeding. He seemed very concerned. He told me that he had called a neurosurgeon that was expected to arrive any minute.

I looked at my wife and told her that I felt better than I had felt earlier. I reminded her that my symptoms were still much less severe than with my previous hemorrhage. I was confident this was a minor blip. I remember saying to my wife, "I am a little worried but I am not panicked."

A few minutes later, the neurosurgeon arrived with the following message:

> You have had a serious bleed in the pons area of the brainstem. I want to admit you to the hospital today. I don't know how long you will have to stay. Your activities will be limited until we make sure the bleeding has stopped.
> The pons area of the brainstem is the worst possible place to have a brain hemorrhage. Frankly, I am surprised that your symptoms aren't more serious. You have survived the bleeding and are still in pretty good shape. You are a very lucky man.
> But, we will need to remove the source, because the next time this bleeds you may not be so lucky. This will be very risky brain surgery. Given the location of your bleed, you could become paralyzed, or become unable to speak - and there is a chance you may go into a coma or even die if we don't remove this soon. But if we don't do surgery, these things are more likely to happen.
> The problem with the pons area of the brainstem is that every millimeter counts. Doing surgery there is something that neither I nor any other Doctor in Dallas, Texas is qualified to do. This is something that you will want only the finest neurosurgeon to consider.
> I plan to refer you to the world's best neurosurgeon in Phoenix. He has done many successful operations in this area of the brain. Even then, there is no guarantee that you won't suffer permanent neurological damage from the surgery.
> This is very serious.
> I will check on you again tomorrow morning to see how you are doing.

After he left I turned to my wife and said, "Now I'm panicked." I was actually more than panicked – I was scared to death.

I was in a hospital bed for a few days. Following that, it took me nearly six months at home to fully recover. I did a lot of thinking and reflecting – as anyone would do. I realized that life is not forever and that it can be snatched away in an instant.

There were a number of things I decided I *needed* to do when I got well. I made a list: 1) tell my sons that I loved them more often; 2) play golf in Ireland; 3) take my wife back to England to visit friends, etc., etc., etc. Miraculously, I recovered and did not require surgery. It took me months to get 'back to normal' but today I'm as good as new.

One of the things on my list of things I needed to do was to write a book on leadership. What follows is the result.

Introduction

"The only real training for leadership is leadership."
- Anthony Jay

How many times have you heard someone say, "My kids didn't come with an instruction book." How true! Those of you who have children know that raising them is pretty much a trial and error process. Sure, there are books and magazines that provide advice and you can try not to make the same mistakes that your parents made. But no one can tell you what to do, step-by-step. It's impossible. Every child is different. Every environment is unique.

This is also true with leadership. People are thrust into leadership positions with no instruction manual – no "how-to" book, if you will. True, there are "management" classes and books. Even though management and leadership are two very different things, good management principles can help you be a better leader. If you are lucky, you have worked for a good or excellent leader and you have learned from that person. You may have also worked for a leader who wasn't as good – and you have learned what *not* to do from them. But, these are only guides. Most leaders must figure out what to do and when to do it on the fly.

I recently read Bobby Jones' autobiography which he wrote at the age of twenty-five. Bobby Jones was a great golfer! Some say he was the greatest golfer, ever. He started playing tournament golf at the age of 13. By age twenty-five, he had won several major golf tournaments including the United States Open twice, The United States Amateur Championship twice, and the British Open. Bobby Jones acknowledged that it was odd that a person would write their autobiography at the young age of twenty-five. He says he decided to write the book because he felt he had *a lot of experience* playing tournament golf.

That's the way I feel. I have a lot of experience as a leader. I started working at the age of 12. I worked my way through high school and college doing a variety of blue-collar jobs.

But, immediately after I graduated from college, I became a leader. Day one, I was a 23 year old, Lieutenant in the United States Air Force and I was in charge of 35 men and women, most of whom were nearly twice my age. I was thrust into my first leadership role. And, I had *no* instruction book.

I have been a leader ever since:

- I have been a leader in four different industries: Government, Oil & Gas, Retail Sales, and Public Utility.

- I have been a leader in Europe and I have been a leader in the United States.

- I have led small groups of less than 10 people and I have led large groups of several hundred people.

- I have led at all levels of the organization from Supervisor to Manager, to Director, to General Manager and Corporate Officer.

- I have led projects, people, finances, and just about anything else you care to mention.

The point is that I have a lot of leadership experience! The people I've led tell me I'm pretty good at it. In fact, many tell me I'm an excellent leader – a great leader. And, they're not just kissing up, something they know I detest. For many of these people it has been years since we worked together and it is unlikely that we will ever work together again. They are sincerely telling me they liked the way I led them and the way I led our organizations, and they are proud of the things we accomplished together. I consider this the ultimate compliment!

I am writing this book because I have some useful, practical advice to pass along to new leaders and would be leaders. I'm not famous – in fact I'm a very ordinary guy. I have never run a large company and I'm not a billionaire. But I have a lot of practical experience leading people and organizations. In this book, I write down the things I've been told make me a great leader. It isn't a "how-to" book, because, like raising a child, it's impossible to write a "how-to" book on leadership.

I hope you can identify and apply some of my advice. I hope you find much of it intuitive – common sense. But most of all I hope that you will also receive the greatest compliment – that the people you lead will tell you that you are a *great* leader.

Note: The stories in this book are true – some of the names have been changed to protect the guilty.

Chapter One: Know Your Business

"Become an expert in your business – not just your functional area."
– Andy Laudato, Senior Vice President & Chief Information Officer,
Pier One Imports, Inc.

Great leaders compliment their strong technical skills with even stronger business skills.
I have three terrific sons. When my sons were in college each of them asked me for guidance on choosing their major area of study. I gave them two pieces of advice:

- Pick a subject area you enjoy, because you will probably be doing it for it at least 40 hours a week for the next 40 years of your life.

- Don't be a generalist – obtain a specific skill or trade. For example, don't major in general business administration – major in accounting, economics, or finance.

All three of my sons took my advice. My oldest son has used his strong math/statistics background to become a fine market researcher. My second son has used his accounting degree to become an excellent internal auditor. And my third son is using his outstanding computer technical skills and degree to become a computer technical specialist.

I believe it is extremely important to have a defined technical skill in today's world. I believed it so much that it was one of the most important pieces of advice I gave my sons when they asked, "How do I decide what my college major should be?"

But if you want to be an excellent leader, if you want to be a great leader, it's not enough to be an expert in your field. *You must also be an expert in your business.* Your goal should be to be the best expert in your business!

For most of my career I have led Information Technology organizations (computers, telecommunications, networks, databases, etc.). However, I am proud to say that no one has ever confused me for a "computer techie." I am always pleased when my manager, my peers, and others say, "Les is a business person, you know, not a technologist."

Do I have technical skills? Yes. Do I need these skills to do my job? Absolutely!

But, in order to be an excellent leader, I must also be an expert about my business. The better I understand my business's strategy, the better I can use this to formulate the right strategy for my part of the organization. The better I understand the challenges facing my business and our industry, and the better I understand our business objectives the more successful I will be in aligning my department's tasks and objectives to support these. The better I understand all of this the better I will be able to communicate it to others in my organization, thus giving a broader meaning and purpose to their every day work. My advice is simple: As a Leader, be a business person first and a functional specialist second.

One thing I do to reinforce this is to start every meeting with a high-level business review. For example I might start my weekly staff meeting by saying:

We are on target to make our $1.95 earnings per share target this year; however we all need to focus on two things for the remainder of our fiscal year. First, we must control our expenses and make sure we hit our revised budget projections. Second, we need to make sure our distribution centers operate at peak efficiency. These are the two things that can make or break our year, financially. Now what can we do to support them?

Bear in mind that I am a computer guy talking to other computer people. There aren't a lot of bits and bytes in this opening statement, huh?

Seize every opportunity to tell your staff what's going on in your company's business. Every department meeting, every staff meeting, every luncheon should begin with a discussion about the broader business perspective. It will help them to focus on what's truly important – that day, that week – which will make them a better organization.

One further piece of advice: Lead your part of the business like it's a part of the overall business organization – not a separate functional area. I've seen this missed in all functional areas, but my functional area, Information Technology, is admittedly one of the worst. Too often computer professionals are enamored with their technology toys – it's oftentimes necessary to challenge them and ask what business purpose a new piece of computer hardware or a new high-speed network will bring.

Great leaders are business people first and foremost. Successful leaders strive to become their organization's best business and industry expert. They understand their business' goals and objectives and structure their department's work to support them. They understand the challenges facing their industry and they help design solutions. Successful leaders demonstrate their business knowledge by communicating in business – not technical terms. They start every department meeting with a short business discussion, and consider it a good thing when someone calls them a good business person.

Chapter Two: Surround Yourself with the Very Best People

"People are not your most important asset. The right people are."
-Jim Collins, *Good to Great*

"The lifeblood of our industry is not capital equipment, but human capital."
- Bill Gates

I don't think it's possible to be a good leader – let alone a great leader – without hiring good people. In fact, I think the opposite is true. I have known many intelligent men and women who made the mistake of thinking they didn't need a strong supporting cast. The truly smart leader will recognize that no matter how intelligent and capable they may be, they can be *even* better when surrounded by the very best people.

Arguably the most prominent leader in the free world is the President of the United States. Once a President is elected, their first priority is to select a cabinet. Some of our most successful Presidents were those who selected the best people for their cabinet. George Washington chose people like Thomas Jefferson and Alexander Hamilton. John F. Kennedy chose his brother Robert Kennedy, and Robert McNamara. Ronald Reagan had great people like Casper Weinberger, Donald Regan and Alexander Haig. Our current President, George W. Bush, chose excellent people like Donald Rumsfeld, Colin Powell and John Ashcroft.

In sports, a coach always puts his best team on the field. He hires the best possible assistant coaches and staff. The higher up you go in sports, the more paramount this becomes. Can you imagine a successful head coach in the National Football League settling for anything other than the best possible players and coaches? Can you imagine George Steinbrenner, the owner of the New York Yankees, not acquiring the best possible talent for his baseball team?

All leaders should adopt the same attitude as the President of the United States or the head coach of a professional sports team. Our first priority should be to select our staff from the very best people available. As Bill Gates has said, "A top performer can improve the average revenue 100 times. Even using a more conservative 10 times per employee figure, the results to your company's bottom line would be huge."

The people we hire should be capable of replacing us. The ultimate leader is one who is willing to develop employees to the point that they eventually surpass him or her in knowledge and ability.

I am a Chief Information Officer. I am proud that I have hired people who were capable of becoming Chief Information Officers. In fact, four of my former direct-reports are Chief Information Officers today, and three of the four achieved this when they were in their early thirties.

When I worked at The Limited, one of the largest specialty retailers in the world, we were encouraged to hire our replacements. At the time, The Limited was growing very, very fast creating loads of promotion opportunities. The company made it clear that the only way a person could get promoted was if they had hired and trained someone else who could take over their job, freeing them to move up the organization. If you hadn't done this, the promotion went to someone else who had.

We should hire employees who are at least as good as we are. If possible we should hire employees who are even better than we are. I once interviewed a person for a position in my organization. As is my practice, I asked this person's potential peers to also interview the candidate. Afterward we convened to discuss the candidate. One of my people got me aside and said, "Les, this guy is very bright and very ambitious. If you hire him, he will be after your job." I simply said, "Good." I knew right then and there that this guy was the right person for the job.

As Leonard Lauder, chairman of the Estee Lauder Companies said:

> I started to hire people I knew were better than I was in certain areas: Carol Phillips to work on Clinique with Dr. Norman Orentreich, and Bob Worsfold, who started our international business. I paid him 30 percent more than I was earning; it was one of the best investments we ever made.

It's easy to say, "You should hire only the best people." How do you put this into action? I recommend the book: *Topgrading: How Leading Companies win by Hiring, Coaching and Keeping the Best People*, by Bradford D. Smart. The book talks about filling every position in an organization with an "A" player, and it provides practical advice on how to distinguish between "A," "B" and "C" players.

Here are some of the things I look for when trying to determine if a person is an "A" player:

> **Intelligence.** Not everyone in the organization needs to be a genius, but everyone you hire should be of above average intelligence.
>
> **Individual Problem Solving Ability.** The best people solve problems and get things done, while others throw their hands up and cry for help or sympathy. The very best people bring you solutions – not problems.
>
> **Group Problem Solving Ability.** The very best

people have the ability to work and play well with others; the ability to be a good team player.

Ambition. I'll take someone with high ambition and above average intelligence over a genius with low ambition any day.

Passion. The best people are passionate about their life and their work. When interviewing a candidate for a job, ask someone who flipped burgers part-time at McDonald's during college, about that job. Take the person who says, "I was the best burger flipper in the state," over the person who says, "I hated that stupid job."

Communication Skills. The very best people can communicate clearly and succinctly.

Technical Skill. Every job has a technical component and the very best people have good technical skills.

Culture Fit. Good people will be even more effective if they share your company's values and beliefs.

I use these attributes to evaluate incumbents as well as potential new hires. The same attributes apply in either case.

Twice in my career I was fortunate enough to work in organizations that had formal programs to assess such skills and abilities. If your organization doesn't have a formal program, you must develop your own method of assessing whether employees and potential employees are A-players.

One mark of a great leader is that they make very few hiring mistakes. Another attribute of a great leader is that they have very low employee turnover. Hiring the very best people can help you achieve these marks.

Chapter Three: Expect People to Achieve More than They Can

"The great leaders are like the best conductors – they reach beyond the notes to reach the magic in the players." – Blaine Lee, The Power Principle

I start out every relationship in my life believing the best in people. I believe that:

- Everyone is good and that everyone has good intentions.
- Everyone is capable of doing good things.
- Everyone wants to do good things.

They have to work really hard to prove me wrong.

Professionally, I also assume that everyone is capable of doing good things. In fact, I assume they intend to do great things. I set high expectations for them, and I have faith they will achieve them. According to one person, who worked with me, "I always felt that you believed I was able to accomplish more than I thought I could. My desire to live up to your expectations helped me to be the best I can be."

One thing is for sure. If you set *low* expectations for individuals they will probably achieve them. The opposite is also true. If you set *high* expectations for individuals they will probably achieve them, as well. I like the story about the guy who said he believed he would *never* win the lottery.

"How often do you play," his friend asked.
"I never play," he said.
"Indeed, it is pretty hard to win if you don't play,"
his friend said.

If we don't expect good things to happen, they probably won't. If employees are not in the game, they never play or win. Typically, whatever you expect from someone – they will reciprocate with their results.

One way to set an overall positive tone is to identify those in your organization with "high potential." These are the people who have the ability to eventually move into your job, or even your supervisor's job. Take them to lunch and tell them how positive you feel. Say: "You are one of the best and brightest people in our company, and I have high expectations of you. I believe, someday, you will be doing my job and I will do everything I can to help you get there – sooner rather than later." This accomplishes two things.

First, it provides positive feedback – and this is very important.

Second, it lets your best employees know it's OK for them to produce results that demonstrate they are capable of replacing you. It lets them know they can do their very best job without threatening you.

Be sure to form your own opinions about people – don't let others influence you, as they surely will try to do. I learned this in my very first leadership role. I was a Second Lieutenant in the United States Air Force and was assigned to Air Force Global Weather Central in Omaha, Nebraska. The Captain who I was replacing sat me down to pass along some wisdom.

He reviewed each of the 35 men and women in my organization, and he told me how good or bad each one was (in his opinion). He told me their strengths but he mostly told me about their weaknesses. I took meticulous notes. I was appreciative of his advice. After all, I was a young Lieutenant in my first leadership role and he was a seasoned Captain with a lot more experience.

But, after reflecting on the conversation, I made a wise choice. I cleared my head of all the negatives, folded the notes up and put them in my bottom desk drawer. I decided not to look at them again for several months – and I began forming *my own* impressions about the 35 men and women working with me.

About six months later I pulled the notes out of my desk drawer and read them with great interest. It turned out that my assessment of people and his assessment of people were very different. Some of the worst people in his view had become some of my very best. And, only one of the thirty-five people had disappointed me. Nearly half of the thirty-five had disappointed him.

I reflected on this a long time. How could this be? Was I too easy? Were they pulling the wool over my eyes? In the end, I asked one of them. I told them flat out that the Captain had given them a bad review. I told them that I, on the other hand, thought they were doing a great job. I asked them if they could explain the difference. Their answer was simple:

> You let me know that you expected me to do great things, and you gave me a chance to do them. The Captain didn't treat me that way.

Great leaders assume people are capable of doing great things. They set high expectations for their employees and they aren't surprised when they achieve them. Great leaders aren't afraid to hire someone who is capable of replacing them – or even capable of replacing their manager. Successful leaders are not threatened by their subordinate's outstanding performance. And great leaders form their own opinions about people in their organization – they don't rely solely on someone else's judgment.

Chapter Four: Remove Obstacles and Get Out of the Way

"If you can find a path with no obstacles, it probably doesn't lead anywhere."
- Frank A. Clark

"To refrain from giving advice, to refrain from meddling in the affairs of others, to refrain, even though the motives be the highest, from tampering with another's way of life – so simple, yet so difficult for an active spirit. Hands off!"
- Henry Miller

Once you have surrounded yourself with the very best people you should remove obstacles that prevent them from being successful. And then – get out of their way! Let them do an excellent job.

I use a three step process as follows:

Communicate Direction. I discuss **what** needs to be done and **when** it needs to be completed. I seek feedback from those who will be managing and doing the tasks. I Ask the following questions:

- Is the objective achievable?

- Is the timeframe reasonable?

- What can I do to help you?

Remove Obstacles. I ask employees what obstacles they see that will prevent them from being successful.

Removing obstacles is something you, as the leader, are uniquely able to do. If funding is an obstacle, you control the budget. You can decide when to shift spending from one area to another. You can decide whether to overspend and explain it as a justifiable budget variance. If the team needs more people, you can authorize them to hire additional staff or to use employees from other areas of the organization. If the obstacle involves problems with a supplier, you have executive level relationships with your supplier's leaders who can remove obstacles in their organizations (See Chapter 20).

In one of my jobs, we installed software from SAP, a German company. We spent nearly two years and millions of dollars in the process. There were many obstacles for me to help remove along the way. Here are three examples:

Software Bugs. The software we installed was an early release and had some program "bugs." Once we discovered the bugs, the process to fix them was taking too long, putting our target implementation date in jeopardy. My project team asked for my help. First, I visited Germany, where the programmers lived and worked, and presented our issues face-to-face. Second, I established a weekly conference call with the German programmers to review progress on our bug fixes. Finally, I visited the programmers in Germany every few months, thereafter, to keep our problems in the forefront and to maintain a personal relationship with them.

As a result, our bugs got fixed more quickly and we were able to complete our project on schedule. SAP executives told me later that I knew more German programmers and more of them knew me than any other customer they'd ever done business with.

System Performance. We had everything ready to go when we discovered that the software would not process our large data volumes. Some program routines ran excessively long (days rather than hours) whereas other program routines would not run at all. We were simply throwing more data at the software than it was designed to handle.

Again, the project team asked for my help. I made some phone calls and discovered there was one person in SAP, a guy named Juergen Becker, who could help us. I used my executive channels to request his assistance. After a good bit of haggling, arrangements were made for Juergen to travel from Germany to Ohio to work with us on-site. I was told Juergen did not like to travel and that SAP had "ordered" him to Ohio, under duress. It was near Thanksgiving when Juergen made his first trip to Ohio, and my wife agreed to make two pumpkin pies that we presented to Juergen upon his arrival. He had never had pumpkin pie before and he loved it! And he loved the gesture. Juergen would make several more trips from Germany to Ohio before all our problems were resolved – all willingly.

Additional People. Time was running out and it appeared we would not make our target installation date. My project team asked me to give them either more time or more warm bodies. They made it clear they would prefer more people so they could stick to their project timeline. I got them more people. I spoke with SAP and they agreed to supply some additional arms and legs at no additional cost – in a partnership fashion. It was a win-win arrangement. We were able to meet our installation date without increasing our project budget. SAP got an on-time installation and a good referral from me to other potential customers.

Depending on your level in the organization, you may not have the authority to do all these things directly. Sometimes you may need approval from someone higher up. But it's your job, as the leader, to present the business case and to fight for the approval.

Let those with approval authority know they have options. If you cannot complete a task in the timeframe and budget expected, for instance, they can either 1) authorize additional people and/or money or 2) grant you more time. When you can't remove an obstacle, you should reset the objectives and timelines and start anew. Stand firm. Don't attempt to meet the same objective in the same timeframe without removing all the obstacles.

Removing obstacles is seldom a one-time deal. If the task at hand is lengthy or complicated, new obstacles will come up. Set up a communication channel so that you know about and can continue to remove new roadblocks, as they are known.

Get Out of The Way. Once you have removed obstacles that could prevent employees from being successful, it's time to get out of the way and let people do the excellent job you know they can do. Another way to say this is: Remove obstacles and don't become one yourself.

This is a no brainer, right? Not necessarily. I have known many leaders who wouldn't get out of the way.

Take Jennifer, for example, someone I worked with along the way. Jennifer was not the type of leader who got out of people's way – she was the exact opposite. She was a controlling, meddling leader who lacked the basic trust and confidence needed to allow employees to work independently. Jennifer led a group of highly competent, well-educated computer programmers who were quite capable of doing their jobs. But she wouldn't let them.

Her controlling, meddling leadership style is apparent in the following document that she distributed to *all* her employees *immediately* upon her arrival.

The following is for real – no joke.

Jennifer's Expectations

- You will only work on approved projects. My boss or I *must* approve any other projects before work is begun.

- Any changes to project definitions and/or scope must be signed by our users before we do any detail design work or programming.

- Project timelines must be completed using Microsoft Project for projects that have a project definition.

- All documents leaving the department and all

documents that act as official documentation within the department must include the author's initials and date.

- I must sign all change documents.

- I should be notified of any production support problems where systems are down or will be delayed beyond the agreed on expectations of the users.

- All memos leaving the department must be carbon copied to me.

- I want to review all project definitions or memos written by our department before they are shown to users.

- If you will be gone from work for more than one hour during business hours, or will be absent from work for a day, I must be notified.

- If you are absent from work for a day, please change your voice mail to reflect that fact.

- No surprises.

Jaj: 9/26/96

You can imagine how this went over – like a lead balloon. It was a good thing for Jennifer to outline her expectations upfront – employees need to know what to expect from a new manager. But, Jennifer's approach to leading people and organizations left a lot to be desired. Jennifer spent a great deal of time meddling in the affairs of her staff. Nothing got done without her direct involvement. People who worked for Jennifer were frustrated, inefficient, and ineffective. Morale was low, and so was productivity. Jennifer was an ineffective leader.

Granted, Jennifer is an extreme example of a leader who did not get out of the way. But, I challenge you to reflect on her extreme methods for a minute and ask yourself if you sometimes lean a little bit in her direction.

My advice is to stay out of the way. You may want to establish periodic review meetings or written status reports to keep advised on progress. These are fine. But, they should be brief, high level, and to the point.

Don't hover. Don't meddle. And, when it comes to leadership don't follow the National Enquirer's slogan – when it comes to leadership 'Enquiring' minds *don't* always need to know.

The people you lead should be spending their time doing their jobs – not constantly updating you and/or answering repeated questions about how things are going. I've known leaders who remind me of children on a long car trip that continue to ask, "Are we there yet? Are we there yet?"

Consider this – you won't always be around. Sometimes you will take a vacation. You may need to attend to a family emergency. Some leaders think they need to "check in" even on these occasions. They phone back to the office, check their email and voice mail; participate in conference calls – anything to keep them in the loop.

This is a mistake. First, it's not good for the leader. You deserve a real vacation – one without checking email, voice mail, or participating in conference calls. You need to devote your full attention to family emergencies, for the sake of family. But, second, it sends the wrong message to employees. It sends the message that "I don't trust you to do your jobs while I'm away."

If you stay out of peoples' hair on a daily basis and forge a truly independent work force that is able to do things without your constant meddling, they will be better equipped to handle things when you are away. In the end, one of the best measures of a great leader is in the way things run when they are *not* around.

There are some big side benefits to this leadership approach.

The less time you spend trying to manage the work of people who are perfectly capable of carrying on without you, the more time you will have to perform valuable leadership functions.

The less time people spend updating you, the more time they will have to do their work.

This makes for a more efficient organization.

In summary, make sure employees have a clear idea of what it takes for them to be successful, remove any obstacles that will prevent them from being successful and then get out of their way. Let them do the great job you hired them to do.

Chapter Five: Don't Second Guess

"Focus on remedies, not faults."
- Jack Nicklaus

"So many men so many questions."
(Quot Homines Tot Sententiae)
- Terence

If you have surrounded yourself with the very best people and then let them do their jobs, the next step is – *don't* second-guess them.

As a leader, you should want employees to make their own decisions. Asking employees to bring everything to you (something many leaders insist on) means one of two things. Either you haven't surrounded yourself with the very best people or you are a control freak.

Empower employees to make their own decisions. Let them know they don't *have* to come to you first. Just think how much more effective your organization will be if:

Employees can take action directly without always seeking guidance from above; and

You aren't spending time providing guidance on everything that happens.

Individuals will be more effective, you will be more effective, and so will your entire organization.

However, if you empower employees to make their own decisions and then second-guess them, the results will be negative. I knew a high-level leader who didn't allow anyone to make his or her own decision. When employees did make a decision without his consultation, he second-guessed them every time.

This person had 14 direct reports and they had all learned that they needed to come to him before they did anything. He hadn't said it, in so many words. Yet, everyone was afraid to make a decision because they knew if they were wrong he would call them and say, "If you had only checked with me first, I would have told you this was a mistake." On the other hand, if he was involved in the *same* exact decision, up front, and the *same* exact thing went wrong, he would defend that decision to the bitter end.

If you were one of his direct reports, what would you have done? You'd probably have taken every issue to him – you probably wouldn't have made a decision on your own. Why would you take the risk of being second-guessed?

Because everything had to go through him, he worked 60 hours a week – minimum. And he still didn't have enough time to talk to everyone who felt they needed to run something by him. He became a bottleneck. I talked with one of his direct reports who told me that he had been trying to get an appointment to see his boss for a month without success. "I've had four meetings scheduled and canceled. I hate to call him at home, but that's what the other guys do. It's the only way you can get to him sometimes." In the meantime whatever he wanted to talk about was on hold.

Don't be this type of leader. Encourage employees to be independent. Let them know you are ready and willing to help if they need you, but that you trust them to do things without checking with you first.

But, and this is key, you must let people know that it's OK to make a mistake now and then. We are all human and, as such, we occasionally make mistakes. In my experience, you will be a more effective leader if you don't second-guess people on these occasions. If you second-guess them, they will lose confidence and start bringing things back to you. Eventually you will be working 60 hours a week, taking phone calls at home, and eventually you will become a bottleneck.

If someone needs your help – provide it. If someone makes critical mistakes over and over again, deal with it. But, for the most part, you are better off letting a few mistakes slide. The upside in organizational effectiveness is worth it.

Great leaders surround themselves with the very best people, empower them to do their jobs, and then don't second-guess them. Great leaders want employees to make their own decisions. When people are empowered to make decisions, they are more effective, the leader is more effective and the entire organization is more effective. Make it clear that employees don't have to come to you before they act. But, also make it clear that employees can come to you for advice and counsel if they need it. Leaders who second-guess their employees encourage them to bring more things to them, and this can result in organizational paralysis.

Chapter Six: Communicate What to Do – Not How

"Don't tell people how to do things. Tell them what to do and let them surprise you with their results."
- George S. Patton

I once had a manager (we called him Dr. Moonbeam behind his back) who not only told me *what* he wanted done, but then outlined, step-by-step, *how* he wanted it done. This was frustrating! I recall him calling me to his office one time and the conversation went something like this:

> *Dr. Moonbeam*: I would like you to prepare a white paper on our network strategy. Start off with some background on how we have done networking in the past, and then talk about all the new network technologies that are available today. Cover the advantages and disadvantages of each new technology. Be sure to talk up the new digital switching technology I saw at last month's trade show, because that's the one I want us to implement. Then include a short section on the pros and cons of adopting the various new technology options and provide a recommendation that supports digital switching as the way to go.
> (Actually, the "instructions" were much more detailed than this, but hopefully you get the idea)
> *Les:* It sounds like you know exactly what you want,

why don't you just write the white paper yourself?
(I've always been a little brash.)

This was the way Dr. Moonbeam operated. On another occasion he asked me to prepare a cost/benefit analysis on acquiring and selling high-tech telecommunication services to tenants in our 1.5 million square foot, 45 story office building. We were a large company who owned the building and occupied about 2/3 of the space. The remaining 1/3 of the space was leased to a number of smaller companies. These smaller companies could not afford to buy the same state-of-the-art technology that we, the larger company, could buy. And, our size gave us purchasing power that allowed us to buy "excess capacity" at a very favorable rate. In theory, we could buy excess capacity and resell it to our smaller tenants, for a profit, but at a price they could afford. We would make a little money and they would enjoy the benefits of the same sophisticated technology as we used. I loved the concept and was excited about preparing the business case.

This was clearly a business issue – not a technology issue. Dr. Moonbeam was a super-techie who didn't understand cost/benefit analysis and net present value calculations. He respected me because I did. He chose me because I was the only person in the technology organization who had the background, education and experience to perform this type of business analysis. I knew (for a change) that he wouldn't give me a step-by-step checklist of "how" to complete this task, because I knew he didn't know where to start. Great! I could finally tackle something on my own.

All this occurred in the early 1980s and when personal computers were just beginning to find their way onto business desktops. Dr. Moonbeam was very excited about this – a new technology. He and four others in our organization (including me) had the company's first personal computers on our desks, and he was anxious to show upper management what great tools these computers could be for everyone in our business.

So, although he didn't know anything about the nuts and bolts of preparing a cost/benefit analysis, he had a definite opinion on "how" I should use technology to complete the task. He told me to use Visicalc to build a spreadsheet. (This was prior to Lotus or Excel.) OK. I was planning to use my PC and Visicalc anyway. No problem.

I built a huge spreadsheet with all the cost and potential revenue factors. There were many calculations and formulas. It took me a few weeks. The results were positive. It looked like we could make some money and provide benefits to our tenants. I went to his office to present my findings. "That's great," he said. "But, you know there is a new spreadsheet software package that is getting great reviews these days. I'd like you to redo the analysis using this new software. Visicalc is old news."

I gritted my teeth and went back to work, putting all the same numbers and building all the same formulas in this newer and improved spreadsheet package. Of course, the results were exactly the same. But Dr. Moonbeam was happy, because I had used a newer, more modern tool.

A few weeks later, Dr. Moonbeam announced that he had read about yet another new spreadsheet package and he would like me to re-build the model using this tool. That's where I drew the line. I said, "All the numbers and formulas will be the same, and the answer will be identical. What difference does it make what spreadsheet tool I use? It will take me a week to rebuild this thing, and I have other work to do." In the end, we agreed I would use the latest and greatest spreadsheet software on the *next* big project – not this one.

I said earlier that if you are lucky you will work for an excellent leader early in your professional career and you will learn from them. The same thing is true in reverse. Having worked for this person, I learned how frustrating and inappropriate it is for a leader to provide detailed, step-by-step instructions on "how" tasks should be completed. I vowed to never make that mistake.

I let people know *what* needs to be done and *when* it needs to be completed – I don't tell them *how* to do it.

Chapter Seven: Provide Positive Reinforcement (Tons of It)

"I have always said that if I were a rich man I would employ a professional praiser."
-Osbert Sitwell, Wisdom

"The sweetest of all sounds is praise."
-Xenophon

My grandmother was a Kansas farm girl. She used to tell me: "Leslie (she was the only person who called me Leslie), you can attract more bees (for making honey) with sugar than with vinegar." She also used to tell me, "If you don't have something nice to say about someone, don't say anything at all."*

Most people, like bees, react better to sweet things than sour things. They respond better to praise than criticism. And when praise comes from the leader, it means all the more.

Everyone in your organization deserves positive reinforcement – everyone. This includes those who are struggling. In fact, I contend that employees who are struggling need positive reinforcement and encouragement the most. I recall an incident when someone told me they had had a "salmon week." Puzzled, I asked what that meant. The response was that she had worked hard all week long and felt she had made little or no progress – like a salmon trying to swim up stream. Now this was a person in need of some encouragement.

As a leader, I take every opportunity to "brag" about my employees. When someone on my team does a really good job – something special – I tell him or her. And then I tell my immediate supervisor. Hopefully, the next time my immediate supervisor sees them they will pass along praise too. I tell their family how valuable they are to the company. I tell *everyone* about the great job he or she is doing.

When I was in the military and someone in my command was promoted or received an award, a press release was sent to their local, hometown newspaper. Most newspapers had a special section for these events and printed a nice article so everyone back home could see what their native son or daughter had accomplished.

I saw first hand how proud this made them and their family, and I learned from this. Every time I had an opportunity to meet a young airman's parents I told them what a great job their son or daughter was doing and how fortunate we were to have them in our organization. It's a good habit I've gotten into and I still do this today. When I meet someone's spouse, I always tell him or her how much I appreciate the person. And, I always tell them how much I appreciate them – the spouse. Their support of their husband or wife's work is also very crucial.

The military has a saying, "Praise in public – reprimand in private." I would amend that to the following: "Praise a LOT in public – only reprimand when you have to – then always do it in private."

Everyone makes mistakes. Stuff happens. Let's say someone who works in your organization issues a financial report with incorrect information – they make a mistake. I've seen leaders react in one of three ways:

They ignore it – pretend they don't even know about it. (If the mistake has not created a serious business problem this may be the best approach. After all, you, the leader, shouldn't be spending time and energy on trivial issues.)

They say, "I heard **we** (not you) made a mistake yesterday. Don't worry about it – everyone makes mistakes – stuff happens." (This is often the best option.)

They say, "I heard **you** (not we) made a mistake on the report yesterday, and I expect that you will take steps to make sure that *never* happens again." And, they say this in public so others can hear their disappointment.

Many leaders choose option three. In my experience, if someone is confronted by the 'boss' and told that the 'boss' is not happy, they overreact. They become exceedingly cautious, checking and double-checking every detail to make sure they don't make another mistake. This is poor leadership!

If the criticism occurs in front of others, it gets worse. The word spreads quickly, and everyone knows that if they make a mistake, they will also have to answer to the boss. Everyone becomes overly cautious. Everyone takes more time checking and double-checking things before they complete their tasks. This makes for a very inefficient organization.

Now, if the same person makes the same mistake repeatedly, a different tact is called for. But, too often, leaders don't distinguish from the one-off mistake and the habitual poor performer.

I am especially bothered by the way some leaders do performance reviews. Performance reviews usually have a section titled "Areas for Improvement" or "Development Opportunities." These are code words for things that employees are doing wrong – bad things – negative things. Many leaders zero in on this section and spend most of the review telling their employees how they should behave differently and/or where they need to improve.

Consider the following analogy from parenting:

Daughter: (Presenting her report card to her father.) "Dad, I got five A's and one B+ this semester."

Father: "The five A's are fine. But let's talk about why you got a B+ in history and not an A."

Daughter: "But Dad, I got five A's and my B+ in history was very close to an 'A'."

Father: "Yes, but I can't help think that if you had applied yourself you would have gotten an 'A' in History as well."

I believe the "Areas for Improvement" section should be the least important section on the review. It may be important that employees know their weaknesses, but believe me, for most employees you are better off mentioning it briefly. And, you should only mention weaknesses after you have spent far more time telling them about all their good qualities and accomplishments. People should walk out of their performance reviews feeling positive about their work – not feeling beat up. Good leaders turn performance reviews into positive reinforcement experiences.

I lost a job over this once. I interviewed for an executive position at one of the world's largest retailers. I was asked the question, "What do you need to work on? What things do you need to do better?" This was a question I anticipated because it is a standard interview question. I had given it a lot of thought, in advance, so that I would have a good, snappy answer ready. So I gave them my answer as follows:

> I have discovered several weaknesses over my 25-year professional career, either through self-examination or by seeking feedback from others. In each and every case, I have worked hard to overcome these weaknesses. At this point in my career there is nothing that I am actively working to improve.

I was called back two more times for interviews and each time was asked the same question, and gave the same answer. I was told later that I did not get the job because at this company, they believe everyone has faults, and that everyone should dwell on these faults so they will constantly be working to improve themselves and become even better.

I obviously would not have fit into that culture. I prefer to dwell on the positive. I think employees need positive reinforcement on the things they do well, and that receiving this positive reinforcement will encourage them to do other things well.

So provide lots of positive reinforcement. Most employees respond better to positive reinforcement than to criticism and/or veiled threats. Take every opportunity to brag about the people you lead. Praise from a leader means a lot, but praise from the leader's manager means even more. So be sure your manager knows when someone in your organization has done something great.

Everyone makes a mistake now and then. When this happens ignore it unless it's critical. If you decide a mistake is critical enough to discuss with someone, use the pronoun "we" not the pronoun "you." Be sure to distinguish the one-off mistake from the habitual poor performer and treat them differently.

Finally, when doing a performance review, spend 99% of your time on accomplishments, not on "areas for improvement." Turn performance reviews into a positive reinforcement experience.

* My grandmother had a lot of sayings, some of which were quite amusing. For instance, she use to say, "Rats on roller skates" and "for crying in a whisper," when she was amazed or surprised about something.

Chapter Eight:
Communicate Effectively

"Don't knock the weather; nine-tenths of the people couldn't start a conversation if it didn't change once in a while."
- Ken Hubbard

I have worked in several organizations, and one thing is common. Employees *never* believe there is enough communication. Never! Employees never believe they have enough information.

The truth is that most organizations have plenty of communication – maybe even too much information. People receive messages via electronic mail, voice mail, fax, PowerPoint presentations, and occasionally face-to-face. All are attempts to communicate information.

The problem in most organizations isn't a lack of communication. The problem is a lack of *effective* communication.

The following is a list of things I believe good leaders can do to be more effective communicators:

Focus on What's Truly Important. Good leaders sort through the myriad of "stuff" (a technical term) that he or she receives and focus on what is really important. A good leader selects a few important messages to communicate. Every leader will have his or her list of truly important things to communicate. Here are some of mine:

> *Our business is on track (or not) and why.* This provides employees with a broader context for their work.

Our department is meeting its objectives (or not) and why. Be sure to tell them how their work, in particular, is contributing to the overall department's success.

I know what you are working on now and I am looking forward to the positive impact it will have on our business.

I know you did a great job yesterday (or last week). I know this because others have told me how much they appreciate what you did.

Repeat Things Again and Again. When something is *really* important, a good leader repeats it, again and again. In my opinion, for instance, you can never talk enough about your department's vision, goals, and objectives.

Seize Every Opportunity to Communicate. Staff meetings and department meetings are an opportunity to communicate. Brief encounters in the hall are another opportunity. Walking around from desk to desk provides an opportunity to communicate. There is no lack of opportunity. Good leaders use them all.

Begin Conversations on the Light Side. I recommend you begin with some positive reinforcement or with something personal to make sure people are at ease. After this, move into the heavier topics.

Communicate in Simple and Straightforward Terms. I began this chapter by saying that I don't know of a single organization that believes they have enough communication. One reason why employees don't believe they have received enough information is that they don't understand the information they do receive. When communicating with someone, you must talk in a language you both understand. Here are a couple of examples:

One of my early managers had a doctorate degree in Electrical Engineering from the Massachusetts

Institute of Technology (MIT). He was one of the brightest individuals I've ever known. He also talked over everyone's head. He would pontificate for a few minutes and no one understood a word that he said. He was often surprised and frustrated when what he thought he asked for came back totally different. The fact was that most of us were too ashamed to ask him two or three times for direction, feeling we would appear stupid. One day a few of us were talking and we figured out that we were all in the same boat – none of us understood him. I (as the appointed spokesperson) went to him and explained the problem, and asked if he could try to communicate in simpler terms. He received the feedback very well and he began to communicate in a simpler, more straightforward manner.

Jack Welch, the former Chairman of General Electric, once said that the way he could tell when a computer project was going well was by walking into a project review meeting to hear the dialogue. If he couldn't tell the difference between technical employees, business people, and outside consultants he knew things were going well. When these people were all talking a common "business" language he knew the project was on track.

Don't Forget to Listen. Listening is an integral part of communicating. It is even more important than talking. I believe that God gave us two ears and one mouth for a reason. Good leaders listen twice as much as they talk.

Make Sure Your Communication is Interactive. Communication is most effective when it is two-way. If you discover you are doing all the talking, stop and simply say, "Does that make sense to you," or "What are your views on that?"

Communicate Face-to-Face. Face to face is still the most effective form of communication. It's easy to forget this in today's world of electronic messages, faxes, voice messages, and other less personal forms of electronic communication. Stop and ask yourself the following question: Have you developed a relationship with individuals – or their computers?

I recall a conversation with Phil, a person in my organization that went something like this:

> Phil: "I sent Steve a dozen emails last week and he didn't respond to any of them."
>
> Les: "Maybe Steve was on vacation last week?"
>
> Phil: "I don't think so. Steve never responds to my emails and in talking with others, he never responds to their emails either."
>
> Les: "Never? What are you doing about that?"
>
> Phil: "I sent him three more emails this week, asking him why he hadn't responded to my first twelve." (At this point I wanted to remind Phil that the definition of stupidity is doing the same thing over and over and expecting different results. But I didn't.)
>
> Les: "Perhaps sending emails to Steve is not the best way to communicate with him. Have you ever tried making the thirty second trip down the hall to talk with him, face-to-face?"

I know individuals who delete a large portion of their electronic messages based on the author and/or subject line. They don't read the text of these messages. As one person told me, "If the email is from Jim I just hit the delete button because Jim rarely has anything important to say." Similarly, I know individuals who delete voice messages if they are more than a few seconds in length. "I just don't have the time to listen to long, rambling voice messages," they say.

I am a great believer in electronic communication. I was a proponent of voice mail and electronic mail in their early, formative years. Under my leadership, British Petroleum America was the first large company in America to use voice mail and British Petroleum International was one of the first heavy users of electronic mail. And, I still believe they can be an effective way to communicate – especially if they are brief and to the point. But, don't allow electronic forms of communication to replace face-to-face conversation. They are no matches for good old-fashioned face time.

Beware of Selective Listening. The fact that you say something doesn't mean that someone hears it. Someone will only retain something if they are *ready* to receive it. As someone recently said to me, "You don't need a bus schedule until you decide to ride the bus."

Be Succinct. It is human nature to "tune out" when communication is too long. When communicating in writing, try to use no more than one page. If you prepare a lengthy paper, preface it with a short and punchy management summary. We all have enough to read. Others will appreciate you being concise and to the point. It will be *much* harder for you to say what you want to say in one page than in three or four pages, but your message is much more likely to be received if it is short.

The problem with most organizations is not a lack of communication. The problem is a lack of *effective* communications. Great leaders make their communication more effective by selecting what's truly important and focusing their communication on that. If something is really important they repeat it again and again. Great leaders communicate often – they seize every opportunity to talk about company performance, department performance and individual accomplishments. Great leaders communicate in a common language that everyone can understand. They keep their message as short and simple as possible. They listen twice as much as they talk. Great leaders communicate face-to-face with people – not just with their computers. Great leaders are great communicators.

Chapter Nine:
Communicate the Big Picture

"The very essence of leadership is that you have to have a vision."
- Unknown

"Communicate the big picture so that people know what they are doing is important."
- Andy Laudato, Senior Vice President & Chief Information Officer, Pier One Imports, Inc.

One of the most important functions of a leader is to provide focus and direction. There is no shortage of things for all of us to do. Providing guidance on what is important, from a big picture perspective, will help employees keep on track.

I love Dave Letterman. I especially love his Top Ten List. I love it so much I adopted the top ten list as a leadership tool. There are a couple of big differences between my top ten list and Dave Letterman's, however:

I have one top ten list per year, whereas Dave has several each week.

Mine is a list of organization initiatives that are not intended to make you laugh. It's not good if someone laughs at my top ten list.

The reason I do a top ten list is to communicate priorities. To let others know what's important for us to accomplish. I list exactly ten things. There are not nine things. There are not two things. And there are not six things. There are exactly ten important things.

I list exactly ten things for two reasons. First, most employees know about Dave Letterman's top ten list. They can identify with it – they tell their family and friends that, like Letterman, their leader has a top ten list. It's familiar and creates a little fun around what could be a dry topic.

The list is also no more than ten because I believe it's unfair to ask any organization to focus on more than ten important things at a time. How many organizations do you know who have twenty or more key initiatives going on at the same time? I suspect you know many. My experience is that organizations can't do twenty things at the same time, and do them all well. Conflicts arise, people get stressed, and new things come up and get added to the list. The result is that some things get done (although most not well), some things don't get done at all and are deferred to the next year, and some things are scrapped altogether, indicating they really weren't all that important to begin with. But the point is that almost *nothing* gets done really well.

And that's a problem. If you restrict the list to ten or fewer things, they will more likely get done – and they will more likely get done well! *It is much more important to do a few things really well than to do a lot of things poorly.* No one should get credit for how many things they have on their plate – the credit should come for completing important things well.

I consider my top ten list one of the most important things I do each year for my organization. It provides them focus. It lets them know what is expected of them and when it's expected. It becomes a blueprint for the year's work.

This list is so important that I spend at least one month each year putting it together. I use the following process:

I determine my business's priorities and objectives for the coming year.

I do a quick hindsight, and identify things my team or I could have done better over the past year. I don't dwell on these, but it's useful to look for them and try to improve.

I put together a rough draft top ten list and ask my management team to review it and propose changes.

Then I hit the road. I review our draft top ten list with my peers and my internal customers. I ask if we have missed anything. I make revisions, as needed, following these meetings.

I present the final, revised top ten list to my entire department, letting them know that these are the things our business most needs from us in order to achieve success in the upcoming year.

I review the list, along with progress in completing tasks/initiatives, periodically throughout the year, and celebrate successes.

When I present the top ten list to my department, I always tell them that I know these ten things are not the only tasks they will work on. But I let them know that in my mind, and in the mind of other business leaders, these are the most important tasks they will work on and it is important that we do them well. I tell them I know other work will "pop up" throughout the year, and I encourage them to do this other work, as long as it doesn't interfere with getting something on the Top Ten List done well.

In addition to developing a top ten list, I try to give my organization a single focus – something that guides all our behaviors. In several of my leadership roles, the single focus I've picked was "delivering excellent customer service." Information Technology (IT) organizations exist to provide service and support to other business functions. It is important that an IT group understands this and it is important that they treat other departments and functions as their "customers." I like to make the following point to an IT organization: There are two individuals in this world who refer to their customers as "users" – drug dealers and information technology professionals.

Making this statement sends a clear message that I want us to be customer service oriented.

When I worked at The Limited the company had twelve autonomous operating divisions: Lerner, Lane Bryant, Express, Limited, Victoria's Secret, Victoria's Secret Catalogue, Cacique, Abercrombie & Fitch, Structure, Galyans, Henri Bendle, and Bath and Body Works were all part of The Limited Inc. Most of these companies have since been closed or sold, but at the time they were all part of the same large company, and each was encouraged to run their part of the business as they saw fit. As a result, each had a different point of focus. Some chose to focus on top-line sales. Others focused on gross sales margin. Still others focused on net sales margin.

The CEO recognized this was a problem. He wanted all divisions to focus on the same thing – top-line sales. He communicated this to all employees and began an internal promotion campaign to let everyone know that their focus was to drive top-line sales. He called the internal promotion "The Main Thing." Once a week, for several weeks in a row, every Limited executive received a trinket or gadget of some kind that said, "The Main Thing is The Main Thing is The Main Thing." And, everyone knew the main thing was top line sales. The CEO also instituted an additional employee bonus program that rewarded employees for exceeding their top-line sales goals. Needless to say, top line sales improved dramatically.

One of the most important functions in leadership is to provide focus and direction. Successful leaders select a few high-impact things for their people to accomplish each year. They concentrate on how well these things get done – not on how many things get done. In addition, great leaders select a single focus or theme for their organizations: something that will guide all their work for the coming year.

Communicating the big picture is important. It provides focus to people's work and frames that work in a broader context. Near the end of this book I present my top ten suggestions for being a successful leader. And, Communicating the Big Picture is on the list.

Chapter Ten: Be Egalitarian

" We hold these truths to be self-evident that all men are created equal; that they are endowed by their Creator with certain inalienable rights; that among these are life, liberty, and the pursuit of happiness."
- US Declaration of Independence

Did you ever notice that "boss" is a four-letter word? It implies that employees *must* do things just because you tell them to – that you have the right to "boss them around." I don't treat the people in my organization this way and I believe no leader ever should.

I think it is important that employees know you are working *with* them. This is much more important than employees knowing they work *for* you – something they already know. It is important that they know *their* goals and objectives are *your* goals and objectives. If they know this, they will be much more likely to consider *your* business goals and objectives to be *their* business goals and objectives.

The dictionary defines egalitarian as follows:

egalitarian
    adj : favoring social equality; "a classless society" n
    : a person who believes in the equality of all people the opposite of an elitist.

I took this approach to leadership on the first day I became a leader. I was a twenty-three-year-old Lieutenant in the United States

Air Force. The military tells its men and women that they *must* respect and obey their superior officers. I just couldn't buy this. Respect is something that must be earned – not dictated. And, although I firmly believe that there are good reasons why military soldiers and sailors must follow the orders of their superiors during battle, the bulk of military life is not spent at war, but keeping the peace. Officers are also not permitted to "fraternize" with enlisted men and women. I became good friends with my enlisted men and women and spent time getting to know them. Occasionally we had a drink together or shared a meal. Sometimes our families got together to do something fun. I did this because I liked and respected them as individuals. I did it in spite of the fact that it was all forbidden according to military doctrine!

In spite of "breaking" all the military relationship rules, I was a very successful military officer. I was a General's aid. I was appointed a regular officer at the earliest opportunity. The Air Force selected me to attend graduate school on their nickel and obtain two Masters Degrees. I received the most prestigious assignments. I was awarded a Meritorious Service Medal and an Air Force Commendation Medal. These are things that go to the most successful and highest potential officers. In my case, I was successful in large part because I worked with my men and women and afforded them the same courtesy I expected them to give me.

I believe it is very important that employees know you are working *with* them. How can you demonstrate this? How can you make this come to life? Here are a few things I do to let employees know I am working with them.

Sit Somewhere Other Than at the Head of the Table. In meetings, it is customary for the leader to sit at the head of the table. I prefer to sit somewhere in the middle. It makes everyone feel more like I'm a part of the team.

Make Room for Everyone at the Table. Let's say you are in a meeting with 15 other people and there are only 12 chairs at the table. There are also a half dozen other chairs along the walls, but not at the table. Ask the 12 at the table to "squeeze up" and invite those along the wall to join you at the table.

Encourage Upward Delegation of Tasks. As a leader you should delegate many tasks. Most leaders understand how to delegate tasks down the organization. I encourage those who work for me to delegate tasks up to me, as well. Sometimes I have more time or more skill for a task than someone who works for me. Why not allow them to assign that task to me?

Use the Pronoun "We" Not "You" When Communicating Tasks. I like to say "we" need to accomplish a task – not "you" need to accomplish a task. This communicates that you and other members of your team are with them. Of course, you must be willing to live up to that.

Get Your Fingernails Dirty. And, be willing to wear some calluses on your hands. I believe all leaders should work.. I recall the story of the child in England who asked her mother, "Mummy, what does the Queen do?" To which the mother replied, "She Queens." I also remember a non-commissioned officer in the Air Force who, when one of his men called him sir (a title normally reserved for officers) said, "Don't call me sir, I work for a living." Leaders who also work send a strong message to others in the organization that they can roll their sleeves up with the best of them.

Seek Input on Key Decisions. Ask for employees' input on major issues. Encourage and be responsive to good ideas from all levels in the organization. Give credit for good ideas to those who deserve it.

Say, "A Person Who Works with Me". Let's say you and Mike Bowman, a direct report, are out for lunch and you encounter an acquaintance – someone that does not work with you. First, be sure you introduce Mike to your acquaintance. Not doing so is rude. When you make the introduction say, "This is Mike Bowman, someone who works *with* me."

Be a Team Member Sometimes. Just because you're the leader doesn't mean you have to *always* lead. Allow someone else to lead important initiatives, and support them as a team member. Be careful not to slip back into the leadership role by taking over meetings and/

or assigning tasks – remember your role for this initiative is one of support.

Serve While Leading. When in combat, military officers eat meals second – only after the enlisted men and women have been fed. At The Limited and at Atmos Energy, executives cook hamburgers and hot dogs at company picnics and serve meals to other employees at company events. This sends a strong, symbolic message that leaders can also serve.

Consider the Message Your Personal Office Space Sends. Some leaders sit in offices as large as some employees' apartments, equipped with mahogany furniture, paneled walls, and lavish carpet, and on, and on. On the other hand, most of their employees work in "cubes." This sends the message that leaders are somehow more important than non-leaders. My advice is to locate your office in the middle of your department, adjacent to your team members – resist moving to the "executive suite." And make your office as non-lavish as possible. I've even seen some senior leaders work in larger cubes, giving up their walls and doors.

Don't Demand the Latest Toys. Some leaders want (demand) all the newest and best technology – the latest and greatest laptop computer, Palm Pilot, cell phone, etc. – every six months, when they are available. Ask yourself if you are getting your job done with your current technology? Is there someone else in your organization that needs an upgrade more than you? Consider what an example you can set if you defer your upgrades to someone who works for you so they can be more productive.

Share Your Space. Regardless of how egalitarian you try to make your office space, it is still your space. Many employees will view your space as "hallowed ground." My advice is to make your space available to others in your group. When you're out of town or in a long meeting, let your assistant know it's OK for others to use your office to conduct meetings and/or house temporary visitors. Space is usually at a premium in corporations. Making your space available will also help ease the crunch.

When I was at The Limited, I opened my home up every year for a Department Christmas party. Everyone in the department, plus their wives, and their children were invited. (One year we had 200 men, women and children.) There was food, non-alcoholic drink and lots of fun. I was talking with someone about this recently and they said:

> My son still refers to you (ten years after the fact) as my boss. This is because of the Christmas parties you had at your home. It clearly made an impression on him. I thought it was great that you opened up your entire house for a party like that.

Share the Perks. Leaders are often offered perks that others in the organization don't have access to – things like tickets to sporting events, small gifts from vendors, etc. My advice is to be generous. Pass some of these along to others in your organization. I was once invited to play golf at a very exclusive golf course. The vendor extended the invitation to me, only. I knew that Jim, a person who worked for me, had wanted to play golf at this course for a long time, so I asked if he could join us. The vendor explained that this event was for Corporate Officers only. Jim was not a corporate officer. I declined the invitation saying I would play only if Jim could join us. Jim and I both received an invitation the next day.

Solicit Upward Appraisals. Most organizations have an annual performance review process where leaders rate subordinates on how they performed over the past year. My advice is to turn the tables and ask employees to also evaluate your performance. If you have built a good relationship with people you will get some good comments. Some of the best advice I've received on becoming a better leader has come from those who worked for me.

Old style, autocratic or hierarchical leaders are out. Successful modern-day leaders need to be egalitarian. Employees need to know their leaders are working with them, not just that they are working for them. As one former employee recently said, "I remember a time when we were working together and you made a point to swing around the table in your office to sit directly next to me, so we could work together. That meant a lot to me."

Chapter Eleven:
Don't Tolerate Kissing Up

"When they discover the center of the universe, a lot of people will be disappointed to discover they are not it."
- Bernard Bailey

Some (I think too many) leaders relish attention. They love to hear their praises sung. They adore flattery. And, guess what. If that's what they want, that's what they will get. Employees pick up on this right away. When rewarded by flattering the leader, they will do more of it. Others will see they have been rewarded, and soon, everyone (except those with the highest integrity and principles) will be kissing up.

You know the signs – beware! Someone tells you that you look like you've lost weight. You celebrate a big birthday (the big Four-O for instance) and a subordinate says you have the energy and looks of a person much younger. Someone *always* sits next to you in meetings. Another person brings you a cup of coffee – with lots of cream and sugar, just the way you like it. Employees telling you what they think you want to hear – just to please you.

I detest brown nosing, and everyone who has ever worked for me knows it – because I tell him or her. I accept and welcome genuine compliments with a smile and simple thank you, but any attempt to influence me beyond that with flattery will not be well received.

I relish the leadership training and experience I received in the military. I was lucky enough to be a General's aid in one of my assignments. I was very young, and still a very junior officer, but because I was the General's aid, I was allowed to sit in his staff meetings with very senior officers.

One Monday morning the General was conducting his regularly scheduled staff meeting. He opened by saying he hoped everyone had enjoyed his or her weekend. One colonel responded that he had spent his weekend in the office working. He said this expecting the General to be impressed and pleased. After all, he had been so dedicated that he had, by his own account, spent his entire weekend working rather than enjoying time with his family. Recognizing this as an obvious attempt to kiss up, the General responded saying:

> If you were working over the weekend it was by your own choice – there are others in this organization that could have helped you get your work done last week. I want everyone in this room to spend time with their families on weekends. God knows we all work enough hours during the week.

This sent several important messages:

> The colonel had scored no points by publicly declaring his weekend work experience.
>
> Others got the message that they would also not score points by kissing up.
>
> The General was concerned about the man's lack of time with his family, which he considered to be just as important as the job.

On another occasion, when I worked at a major specialty retailer, the executive team met once a month, on Saturday morning, to review the past month's business. This was a great opportunity for us to discuss what went right and what we could have done better in a relaxed, Saturday morning, empty office atmosphere. Typically only the top executives attended these Saturday morning meetings. It was not commonplace for others to work weekends, except for extraordinary circumstances.

However, one department head ordered his entire department to show up for work on these Saturday mornings. He wanted the other executives to *think* his department was working really hard. He thought the other executives would assume that his department was so dedicated they worked every Saturday morning – which they didn't. When employees balked, he offered them double time off during the regular working week for showing up on one Saturday morning each month. What an obvious example of kissing up. What a poor example of leadership!

If kissing up is bad, why do people do it? Vanity is a human trait that is easily exploited. Too often employees are rewarded for kissing up to the leader, and people do what they are rewarded for.

So what's the harm? I believe employees should be rewarded for the things that make organizations successful. There is nothing about kissing up to the leader that makes an organization more successful. Discourage – not encourage – kissing up. You will be a more respected and successful leader.

Many leaders relish attention. If that's what a leader wants then that's what he or she will get. Great leaders don't reward flattery – they discourage it. Great leaders respond to genuine compliments with a simple, "Thank you."

Chapter Twelve: Have the Courage to Make Tough Decisions

"A true leader has the confidence to stand alone and the courage to make tough decisions."
- Source Unknown

"Courage is resistance to fear, mastery of fear – not absence of fear."
- Mark Twain

Leaders must make tough decisions. That's why they pay them the big bucks, right? Let me give you an example of a really tough decision I made.

I was a Captain in the United States Air Force stationed at Offutt Air Force Base in Omaha, Nebraska. I was responsible for voice, message, and command and control telecommunications. Late one Wednesday afternoon, the first week in February, I received word that an airman, on temporary duty from another state, had died from electrocution while digging a trench for a new communications cable. I was appointed to handle his personal affairs.

After reading the manual, I discovered that my first order of business was to gather all his personal effects – clothing, jewelry, papers, cards, and letters. The manual said that I should inspect everything thoroughly before returning it to his loved ones. The manual said I must open every box, drawer, and storage locker. I was supposed to review every item in his wallet before sending anything back. The reason was to make sure I didn't return anything that would cause the family pain or embarrassment. The manual even gave an example – pornography. It explained that someone's mother or wife may not know or approve of pornography and it advised that I destroy any such items as to avoid causing undo additional hardship.

I went to his room at the barracks and cleaned out his closet and drawers. I found a gift-wrapped Valentines Day present for his wife. Valentines Day was less than two weeks away. This caused me to think. Would receiving the gift, after her husband's death, cause more pain than good? Should I unwrap the gift to make sure it was not something vulgar? In the end, I determined the gift was private and that his wife would find joy – not sorrow – in receiving it. I returned it with his other possessions – but the gift was unopened.

Several weeks later I received a note from the airman's wife thanking me for my efforts to return her husband's items, and thanking me, especially for passing along the Valentine gift. I made the right, tough decision.

Leaders face many tough decisions, but some of the toughest involve personnel issues. The next chapter is about making the decision to let someone go. There are other personnel decisions that can be just as tough – especially if you, the leader, are genuinely interested in and care about your people. Let's look at another example:

I was the Chief Information Officer for a prominent retail company. I had surrounded myself with the very best people and had a fantastic team of dedicated men and women who were accomplishing great things for the business. One day, my head programmer came to me to tell me that he was leaving the company to become a Chief Information Officer at another retailer. I was thrilled! He was young, bright, and hard working. He had great leadership skills and, in my opinion, was certainly ready to take on this new challenge. I wished him the best, and made sure he knew that, if he needed any advice, he was welcome to pick up the phone and call me.

Now the challenge – picking his replacement. I decided right away that there was no reason to go outside the company. I had a strong team and there were three strong, internal candidates for the job: Janice, Frank, and Jim.

Janice had been with the company for twenty years and she knew our systems better than anyone in my department. Janice had been particularly helpful when I joined the company. She was one of my strongest supporters and allies in my early days. She had been considered for the head programmer's position more than once (prior to my arrival) and my predecessors had passed her over, choosing someone with less experience and but perhaps more leadership ability. She could definitely do the job, but I wasn't sure she was a candidate to eventually take on my job. Maybe it was her turn?

Frank had been with the company for about ten years, and was on my list of people with high potential. But, Frank was a techie. He had great potential as our future head technical guru, but, in my opinion, lacked the business skills and acumen to lead the programming group.

Jim had been with us only two years. He was much younger than Janice and Frank, and therefore lacked the savvy and experience of a seasoned leader. But, Jim had accomplished great things in his short time with the company. For instance, he had programmed an automatic merchandise replenishment application that increased our sales for blue jeans by twenty percent. He had also led a team of programmers who developed a merchandise planning application that had quickly gained the reputation of being the best in the retail industry. Jim was ambitious. Jim was energetic. Jim had hired some of the very best people I had ever known in his short time with the company. He had good leadership instincts and he was very open to coaching. Jim definitely had the potential to replace me in a few years.

It was a *tough* decision between Janice and Jim, but in the end I chose Jim. I sat down with Frank and Janice, in private, to let them know my decision.

Frank wasn't surprised. In fact, he told me he was relieved. He preferred to remain on a technical career path. Janice, on the other hand, was disappointed, to say the least. When I told her of my decision, she cried. I felt terrible! I made sure she knew that I was extremely happy with her work. I made sure she knew she had been a viable candidate for the job. I told her what a difficult time I had choosing. I told her I didn't consider going outside the company to fill the position, because we had strong internal candidates, like her. I encouraged her to think about it and come back and talk later if she wanted to. We talked again in a couple of days and by then, Janice was fine.

The sequel to this story is that just two years later, Jim left the company. This time, Janice got the head programmer job.

In his book, *Only the Paranoid Survive*, Andy Grove (then President and CEO of Intel) describes the critical decision Intel made in 1985 to shift their product emphasis from memory computer chips to processor computer chips. Intel had dominated the memory computer chip business since 1976, commanding up to 60% of the worldwide semiconductor market share. But in the early 1980s they faced stiff competition from Japanese memory producers, who were producing larger, cheaper and higher quality products than Intel. By 1985, Intel's worldwide market share had dropped to about 40% and Japanese companies commanded the other 60%.

There was a heavy debate inside of Intel about how to respond. Some wanted to build a huge memory chip factory and go head-to-head with the Japanese. Others thought Intel should try to beat the Japanese with technology by engineering and building something the Japanese couldn't produce. Still others thought the company should focus on niche, special purpose memory products.

Intel was losing market share and they were losing money by clinging onto the memory chip business. Andy Grove described the moment when they made the tough decision to get out of the memory chip business and retool the company to produce the best processor chips in the world as follows:

> I remember a time in the middle of 1985, after this aimless wandering had been going on for almost a year. I was in my office with Intel's chairman and CEO,

Gordon Moore, and we were discussing our quandary. Our mood was down beat. I looked out the window at the Ferris wheel of the Great America amusement park revolving in the distance, then I turned back to Gordon and I asked, 'If we got kicked out and the board brought in a new CEO, what do you think he would do?' Gordon answered without hesitation, 'He would get us out of the memories.' I stared at him, numb, and then said, 'Why shouldn't you and I walk out the door, come back and do it ourselves?'

This was a tough decision – to abandon the business that had gotten Intel to the top of the memory chip industry and transform it into a totally new business, with different technology, different manufacturing facilities, different engineering, production, and marketing skills. Had the decision not been made, the company would have surely died a slow death. Instead, Intel became *the* worldwide brand in computer processor chips, and personal computers and servers come banded with the words "Intel Inside."

The next time you are facing a tough decision, it might be a good thing to ask yourself the same question Andy Grove asked at Intel. "What if they replaced me tomorrow? What would my successor do?"

I have made a lot of tough decisions in my leadership career. When in doubt, I try to let my conscience be my guide. "When in doubt, do the right thing" is a topic of a later chapter. But it deserves mention here, as well.

Great leaders have the courage to make tough decisions. Great leaders don't shirk their decision-making responsibilities. Great leaders stand by their decisions with confidence and conviction. Even great leaders occasionally make mistakes. When they do, they admit it and take full responsibility.

Chapter Thirteen:
Deal with Bad Apples – Swiftly

"A true leader has the confidence to stand alone and the courage to make tough decisions."
- Unknown

Making a decision to let an employee go may be one of the most difficult things for a leader to do. And, doing it swiftly makes it even tougher. It is important to note that there are two different points here. First, the best leaders must deal with bad apples. Second, they must do it swiftly. Both points are important.

Sometimes things just don't work out. Sometimes you and one of your employees have to part ways, for the good of the organization as well as the individual concerned. I've done this a few times in my career and it has never been easy. I've always lost sleep over it. Letting someone go affects their family, their life. It just makes you feel rotten. And, if you feel rotten, think how bad the person being let go feels.

Because letting someone go is so tough, many leaders fail. And, I've seen leaders fail both ways. I've seen leaders who won't rid the organization of bad apples and I've seen leaders who will fire someone at the drop of the hat.

I probably lean toward the first type of leader. I try to give employees a fair chance to come around. Sometimes I give them several chances. But, as a leader, if you find someone in one of the following situations, you must act – and you must act quickly:

Someone Who Lacks Competence. You've done your best to surround yourself with the very best people. You think you have all

"A" players. But, you find you've made a mistake. You are willing to tolerate a "B" player, but you discover you actually have a "C" player. The "C" player must go and be replaced with an "A" player.

Someone Who Is Unable to Work and Play with Others. You may have someone in your organization that is a constant source of conflict. They may be an "A" player, but they agitate and irritate others to the point where organizational productivity is hurt.

Someone Who Is Unable to Accept Change. Today's business world is constantly changing. Some people are unwilling or unable to accept change, while others embrace it. Of course, everyone should be allowed to discuss and debate changes, but once decisions are made, those who habitually fight them must go.

Someone Who Clashes with the Organization's Culture. Employees who don't fit an organization's culture will have a negative affect on that organization's productivity and overall happiness. I once knew a senior level leader who was a brash egomaniac. He might have fit well in a Wall Street Financial Trading Company, but he was a square peg in a round hole in our business.

Nay Sayers. People who are spreading bad karma. Something has happened to tick them off and they begin to constantly bad-mouth you, your superiors and the company.

Someone Who is Unwilling to Follow the "Rules." Someone who habitually comes to work late or leaves early. People who don't show up for important meetings, etc.

Someone Who Commits Acts of Theft, Fraud, Etc. Most companies have an employee manual outlining certain acts that are grounds for termination. The trick here is applying these rules fairly and equitably. At one company where I worked, theft of any kind wasn't tolerated. People were fired for stealing something worth 50 cents just as quickly as a someone who stole something worth hundreds of dollars.

These are some of the most damaging people to organizations and it is important that they be dealt with quickly. Consider the following:

Everyone is expecting you to deal with him or her. If *you* know it's not working out then everyone else surely knows it. Not dealing with it undermines your credibility as a leader.

The behaviors above can all be damaging to an organization. The longer these people remain in place, the more damage they can do to an organization, to you and to themselves.

You must act quickly for the sake of the bad apple. Chances are they are not happy. They can't be. If you know things aren't working and everyone else knows things aren't working, do you really think the person doesn't know? I've never let anyone go where it was a surprise. Not because I necessarily did a good job of counseling them or warning them – just because they know. My experience is that someone who is unhappy in one job is ultimately better off in a different job. They are happier in a place where they fit better.

Here are a few more tips on dealing with bad apples:

Don't let someone go on a Friday. They will have all weekend to sit and stew about it. Better to let someone go in the middle of the week.

Don't override your direct reports. Your management team has the right to pick their very best people – just like you had the right to pick them. If one of them comes to you to let you know they need to let someone go, let that be their decision. Of course, you should talk it through and provide any coaching that might be useful. But, in the end, let them know it's their decision – not yours.

No one is indispensable. Oftentimes, when it's obvious that a person needs to move on, their manager will tell me, "but we can't operate without them." That is rarely the case. Even if the person is critical, it is better to rid the organization of the cancer first, and deal with their supposed indispensability second.

Don't be too trigger-happy. This might sound like I am contradicting myself. My advice is still to deal with bad apples *quickly*. But, don't be the type of leader who fires someone just because they rub you the wrong way. Just as others know when it's time for someone to go, they also know when someone is being fired for no good reason. They will rightfully begin looking over their shoulder, wondering if they are next.

Making a decision to let someone go is one of the toughest decisions for a leader to make. Dealing with these people swiftly can make it even tougher. Perhaps because it is so tough, many leaders fail. Some leaders are too quick on the trigger while others can't pull the trigger at all. Just remember, if you know an employee is not working out then it's likely that everyone else knows as well, including the person in question. Everyone is expecting you, the leader, to do something. The quicker you deal with it, the faster everyone can get on with the business of running the business.

Chapter Fourteen: Be A Leader – Not A Kindergarten Teacher

"Difficulties are meant to rouse, not discourage. The human spirit is to grow strong by conflict."
- William Ellery Channing

Individuals don't always get along. It's a fact of life. Sometimes employees have disagreements. Sometimes people do things that irritate their co-workers.

When I arrived at a new job I had four direct reports. Curtis was my Director of Technical Services, Bill was my Director of Operations, Jane was one of my Directors of Program Development, and Tom was my second Director of Program Development.

My butt had barely hit my office chair when Curtis came to me complaining that Jane was making unreasonable demands on his staff. He recommended that I fire her. Next Jane came down to tell me that Bill would not make computer disk space available for her programmers to do their jobs. No sooner had Jane left and Bill came to me to say that Jane was impossible to work with. Jane came back to make sure I knew that Curtis and his group had it "in for her."

What was happening? It was clear that Jane, Bill, and Curtis were not working and playing well with each other. It was also clear that they expected me, their new leader, to resolve their disputes. Frankly I was flabbergasted. They reminded me of a bunch of kindergarten students, going to their teacher, expecting the teacher to settle an argument. They expected me to intervene and become a referee.

I'm afraid I disappointed them. I spoke to each of them, individually, and gave them the same message. "Thank you for telling me about your problems with your co-workers, but I am here to provide direction and leadership to our organization – not to solve interpersonal problems. You and your co-workers are adults. I expect you to behave like adults and work it out!"

Interestingly enough, this is the way I treated my children. If one of my sons had an argument with his brother and came running to me to complain, I told him to go back to his brother and work it out. I think they are better adults today because I didn't teach them they could run to an authority figure to resolve all their problems.

Sometimes my children (and employees who work for me) were not able to work things out. On those occasions, I got everyone in the same room at the same time, and made them talk it out. I do this only as a last resort. Note the words "let *them* talk it out." During these sessions, I play the role of facilitator. I don't offer solutions and I don't try to referee, I simply facilitate their conversation. Sometimes, just making sure they actually have a conversation is what a leader needs to do.

People have a tendency to take every problem to the top. I am amazed at how many times one of my peers has come to me and said something like: "Jim asked Robert for something two weeks ago, and he still doesn't hasn't done it." My immediate response is, "Has Jim talked to Robert about why he is late?" Too often the answer is that they don't know. Even more often the facial response I receive indicates they are disappointed that I am not jumping at the chance to intervene.

I recall a conversation with one of my project managers as follows:

> Project Manager: "Bob told Sally that you and the rest of the executive team are displeased that my project is behind schedule and over budget, and that you are about to replace me with someone else. Is this true?"
> Les: "Do you think this is true?"

Project Manager: "No, I think if you or anyone else on the Executive Team had problems with my performance, you'd be the first to tell me."

Les: "You're right. If I was unhappy with your performance I'd tell you."

Project Manager: "Well what are you going to do about Bob spreading these terrible rumors? He's undermining my authority."

Les: "Nothing. It's up to you to go to Bob, discuss it with him, and work it out."

I encourage direct, face-to-face conversation to resolve conflict. Employees should not expect their leader to solve their working relationship problems. If you respond, people will take more and more of these problems to you and you will become a full-time counselor. If you see a conflict, be proactive. Tell them to go somewhere else and work it out. But, don't allow them to use you to arbitrate everyday problems. Remember that you are their leader – not their kindergarten teacher.

Chapter Fifteen:
Delegate – Both Up and Down

"You can delegate authority, but not responsibility."
- Stephen W. Comiskey

Every management textbook tells you to delegate. Few tell you how, but they definitely think it's a good idea.

I've known leaders who delegated everything. They didn't write memos; they never prepared a presentation; they didn't place their own phone calls; they never scheduled a meeting on their own. They had someone on their staff do these things. In essence, their job was to tell other people what to do. They didn't do any real work – they just led.

I've also known leaders who have trouble delegating anything. They simply can't let go. The two best excuses I hear for not delegating are:

> "It will take me more time to explain it to someone else than to just do it myself."
> "I am more qualified than anyone who works for me."

What's the use in hiring the very best people if you can't grant them the authority to act on your behalf?

So at the one extreme, some leaders delegate everything while at the other extreme other leaders delegate almost nothing. Neither of these leaders is effective. The answer is somewhere in between.

I believe great leaders know how to delegate well. Here are some tips on delegating:

Take Yourself out of the Loop. The best way to delegate is to not be in the loop in the first place. Sure leaders need to understand and be aware of what's going on in their organization. But, not everything that needs to get done needs to come through you. Encourage employees to go directly to others when they need something done. If someone comes directly to me with a work request I frequently say, "Why don't you go talk directly with Sharon? I'm sure she will be happy to help you."

This can be challenging. Everyone wants face time with the leader. They believe their request will carry more weight if they take it to the leader, and the leader gives direction, top down. One time a supplier/vendor demanded a face-to-face meeting with me. My response was, "Talk directly to Andy. He is the decision maker." I told him this over and over again. But this guy just wouldn't take "no" for an answer. So I finally agreed to see him. I also invited Andy.

As I expected, he began to make a pitch that was a waste of my time. There was nothing in his presentation that he couldn't have said directly to Andy. He was also sloppy and a poor communicator which didn't help.

I interrupted and said, "Excuse me. This is not a good use of your time. And, it's not a good use of my time either. Do you realize how many people try to get a piece of my time every day?"

I then began going through my full inbox and started pitching things in the trash one-by-one. "This pamphlet is from someone wanting me to attend their seminar." Trash. "This one is from someone offering me a free software trial." Trash. "This memo is from a consultant who claims he can improve my business by 20%." Clunk.

"As I tried to tell you before this meeting, you are not helping your cause by speaking to me. Andy is the decision maker. Andy has budget authority for his part of the organization. If Andy decides to buy, he'll buy. And here's the kicker – you can't really help yourself by talking directly to me, because I'm not making the decision. But, you *can* hurt yourself by talking with me, because I might see or hear something I don't like. And today – believe me, you've hurt yourself."

Needless to say, this fellow dealt with Andy directly from that day forward.

This sent a strong message to a persistent person that getting to the top was the *not* the key to his success. It also sent a strong message to Andy, reaffirming that he had authority to make decisions without me being involved.

Delegate Meaningful Work. Don't delegate a task just because you find it boring and/or you think it's beneath you. Employees will lose respect for you quickly. If anything, error in the opposite direction. Delegate assignments that will challenge individuals and give them opportunities to display excellence. I was once asked to serve as a member of a due diligence task force, evaluating other companies for potential acquisition. I had experience doing this in other companies and would have been the best choice to represent my department. But, instead, I delegated this to a bright, younger direct report because he could benefit from the new experience and corporate-wide exposure.

Ask, "Who is Best Qualified?" Sometimes you are the best qualified person to do a job. You have the right background, training, and skills. Often times, another person is better qualified. That's the person who should complete the task.

Don't Delegate because you are Overloaded. You are responsible for managing your own workload. You are responsible for making sure you have not taken on too much. If you're overloaded, it's your problem, not someone that works for you. It's OK to ask for help when you are overloaded, but don't just dump things on others and call it delegation.

Allow Employees to Delegate Upwards. I allow employees who work for me to offload tasks to me, if I am more qualified than they are. I also tell employees when I have a "light week" and encourage them to let me help. I've found this is a great leadership tool. It reinforces the concept of giving work to the best qualified person (even if that person is the leader). It promotes egalitarianism. And, it helps keep the workload better balanced.

Delegation is not an easy thing. It's easy to say but hard to do – properly.

Recognize that everyone thinks they will have a better chance of getting something done if the task comes from the top down. Let others know this isn't your style.

Delegate meaningful work to others – not stuff (a technical term) that you or no one else wants to do.

Always consider who is the best qualified to complete a task. Is it you, or is one of your co-workers better qualified?

Manage your own work and don't dump things on subordinates in the name of delegation, just because you're overloaded.

And, encourage others to delegate tasks to you when they feel you are better qualified and/or if they need some short term help.

Chapter Sixteen: Be Decisive

"When you come to a fork in the road, take it."
- Yogi Berra

Great leaders must be decisive. No one respects a wishy-washy leader. In addition, today's fast paced, electronic, information age business demands quick action. Not acting quickly can cost a company big money. Not acting decisively can create lingering doubts in those you work with.

Great leaders are risk takers. They make decisions without gathering *one hundred percent* of the necessary information. And, more times than not, they are right. Is this because great leaders have superior instincts? Do they have super human powers that allow them to sense the proper course of action?

I believe great leaders develop instincts that help them make better decisions. The key word here is "*develop.*" I don't believe great leaders are born with this quality. They learn, through experience, to filter through the information they receive and to make reasonable assumptions about things they don't know. They train their brain to *quickly* assimilate information – weeding through all that's been presented and identifying those things (and only those things) that are pertinent. And then they act.

But, just as important, great leaders understand that, in the real world, there is rarely one right answer to a problem and there is rarely one path to success. They know there are always many ways to get from point A to point B. They know that making a decision, sometimes any decision, is better than not doing anything at all. And they know that they will rarely have *all* the facts and information they need before they have to pull the trigger. When a great leader comes to a fork in the road, he or she takes it. (My favorite Yogi Berra quotation.)

We all remember 9/11/2001; the day Al Qaeda terrorists flew two jumbo jets into the World Trade Center in New York City, another jumbo jet into the Pentagon, and yet another crashed in rural Pennsylvania. Many brilliant leaders emerged from this tragedy, but the one person who stands out in my mind is President George W. Bush. He made critical decisions in the days following these attacks, and few would debate the correctness of these decisions. Do you think he had *all* the information about the Taliban and Afghanistan before retaliating against them for harboring Al Qaeda terrorists? He certainly had some government intelligence, but I would bet money there were many unanswered questions and that he probably received conflicting advice from various people. He took what he had and made the critical decision to attack terrorists before they could attack us again. In doing so, he declared a "war on terrorism" and put other terrorist harboring nations on notice. Others may have begun with further international sanctions and/or diplomacy. Others may have used a word weaker than "war." But President George W. Bush didn't. He made a fast, critical decision to declare war. Hindsight suggests he made the right choice. We may never know how many American lives were saved by these actions.

The military has always taught the importance of rapid, accurate decision making. Military officers are taught that delaying a decision and/or making the wrong decision in the heat of battle can be the difference between victory and defeat. I believe this makes the military one of the best training grounds for leadership skills.

As a young military officer, I learned how to act quickly. I learned to make the right decisions even though I didn't have *all* the information. I learned how to sort out the wheat from the chaff. I give credit to my early military training for developing the good instincts needed to make quick and accurate leadership decisions throughout my career.

Chapter Seventeen:
When in Doubt – Do the Right Thing

"Listen, there is no courage or any extra courage that I know of to find out the right thing to do. Now, it is not only necessary to do the right thing, but to do it in the right way and the only problem you have is what is the right thing to do and what is the right way to do it."
- Dwight David Eisenhower

Leaders make decisions. Others expect them to make decisions. They need their leader to provide direction. But, what if you don't know what to do? What if you have more than enough information but you are still uncertain? My advice is simply:

Do the right thing.
Doing the right thing is never wrong.

I have some first hand experience in making tough decisions by deciding to do the right thing.

When I first joined one the most successful specialty retailers in the world, the company was working to develop the retail business software of the future. Forty-five programmers had been working for three years in a small room away from the everyday business operations – trying to program new computer applications that would revolutionize the specialty retail business. To date they had spent $30 million. The vice chairman, the project's sponsor, was very proud of "his" project. He was eager to see the first new programs become available to the business. And, he was convinced that when all the work was done the company would gain a competitive advantage.

And, that was the problem. Forty-five programmers had been working for more than three years and they had spent $30 million – and not a single new program had been developed. These employees reported to me so I felt obligated to find out what was going on. What I found was troubling. Based on my experience with other software projects, I determined that this one was doomed to failure. The project team had done an excellent job of defining and documenting the business requirements for the retail software of the future. And, one piece of software showed some promise. But the majority of the work had become mired down in an attempt to use "bleeding edge" computer technology. In essence, the company was trying to develop software with technical computer hardware and software before these tools were ready. The project team lacked the skills and/or the ability to overcome this hurdle.

I was the new guy. I'd only been with the company a few weeks. What was I to do? On the one hand, going to the executive sponsor, the vice chairman, to tell him that he had squandered $30 million and that if the project continued he could squander another $30 million and still not achieve his objectives could be political suicide. Others who had been with the company far longer than I assured me it *would* be political suicide. On the other hand, allowing the project to continue knowing the outcome was failure would have been irresponsible of me.

After thinking it through I went to the vice chairman and explained the situation. He was not the kindest and gentlest leader that I've encountered and he clearly let me know he was about to shoot the messenger. I explained that I had reviewed hundreds of software projects while at other companies and I had a good sense when one was off the tracks – and this one was definitely off the tracks. I put the issue in terms that he could relate to. "We know when a buyer purchases $30 million of bad merchandise because customers won't buy it," I said. "We move quickly to mark down the merchandise and salvage what we can. Then we move on. This software project is very similar," I continued. "We know this has been a bad investment because the team hasn't delivered the new software in the timeframe we expected. We have a good solid business requirements document and one piece of software that can be salvaged. The rest needs to be written off and we should move on." He agreed, and less than a week later the software of the future project was disbanded.

I look back on this incident as a defining moment. I don't think I realized how much of a risk I was taking. After I had gotten to know the vice chairman better, I found out he was even meaner than people had told me. But, taking the stand I did was the right thing to do, and it is never wrong to do the right thing.

I have another story about doing the right thing from my days in the retail business. A group of executives (including me) was talking with our Chairman and CEO one day when he told us about making groundbreaking decisions around customers and returned merchandise. When he opened his first store, it was standard retail business practice to allow customers to return merchandise *only* if they had a "good reason" and *only* for a limited period of time. For instance, a customer could return a knit top if they discovered a fabric flaw, but it had to be returned within 14 days. If the store clerk agreed you had a good reason for returning the knit top and you had done so within the two week time frame, you were given a "due bill" to purchase other merchandise in the store – not cash.

The Chairman thought this was wrong and he decided to change the rules. Customers who purchased merchandise in his store were allowed to return merchandise at any time (no sale was ever final) and for any reason. A customer could literally return merchandise years after their purchase – no questions asked. If they had paid cash for the merchandise, they were given a cash refund and not a due bill.

The Chairman explained that he believed that most customers were honest and that they would not take advantage of what seemed to be the right policy around returning merchandise. He believed that if a customer was unhappy with their purchase – no matter what the reason – they deserved a refund. And if that customer had paid him cash, they deserved cash back. "It was the right thing to do," the Chairman said. In changing the rules for his store, he ultimately changed the rules for all of U.S. retail.

What a great example of doing the right thing. What a great example of superb leadership!

Chapter Eighteen: Don't Ask People to Do Something You Wouldn't Be Willing to Do

"It is not fair to ask of others what you are unwilling to do yourself."
- Eleanor Roosevelt

Early in my Air Force career I had the opportunity to be a General's Aide. This was a big deal, by the way. No one got to the General without first going through me. I accompanied him on his travels and sat in on all his high-level strategy sessions. Generals are pretty sharp individuals. Being an aide to one was a great opportunity for a twenty-something year old man to see how a military executive operated.

The General came to me one evening on the last day of a two-week field exercise – war games, if you will. He was pleased at how well the exercise had gone. He explained that many men and women had worked around the clock. Then he said:

> People have worked really hard for me over these past two weeks, and we wouldn't have been successful without them. There are about 100 individuals that I would like to personally thank by sending them a letter. I have scribbled their names and a few notes on this sheet of paper. Would you please draft these letters and have them on my desk first thing in the morning? And, I don't want 100 form letters – I want each one to be personal.

It was 4:30 p.m. on a Thursday. This was in the days before word processors or personal computers. These letters would have to be typed, one at a time, on an electric typewriter. I said, "General, the only way I can have personalized letters on your desk by first thing tomorrow is to work all night." He told me he realized this. He explained that it was important that these individuals receive their letters by the next day (Friday) because he wanted them to receive his personal thanks prior to the weekend. I asked myself, "Is this a reasonable request?" I decided it was. And I said, "Yes sir." I worked all night and he had one hundred personal letters on his desk when he arrived the next day. After making sure he had what he needed, I went home and went to bed.

In another leadership role, executives were required to work one Saturday morning each month. We met from 8:00 a.m. to 12:00 noon to review the month-end financial results and strategize the next month's business. Working Saturday is not something that appealed to me – I'd rather be playing golf or spending time with my wife and children. But, I gladly spent one Saturday a month attending these meetings, because I saw the business rationale. First, Saturday seemed to be the only time we could take four hours to have these discussions. In addition, all executives gave up their Saturday morning for this meeting from the President on down.

I am reminded of a story about Gandhi. People sought advice and wisdom from Gandhi on many matters. One woman brought her son to Gandhi to seek his advice about his hyperactivity. After hearing the woman's case, Gandhi asked to talk with the boy alone for 15 minutes. He then instructed the woman to return home with her son and asked her to come back to see him in two weeks. Two weeks later the woman and her son returned and Gandhi said: "My advice is for your son to eliminate sugar from his diet." To which the mother, somewhat indignantly, replied, "You could have told us that two weeks ago." Gandhi's response was: "No I couldn't have recommended that your son eliminate sugar from his diet two weeks ago, because first I had to eliminate sugar from my diet. I would not ask someone else to do what I had not yet done."

Similarly, I know a family with a diabetic child. The entire family has given up sugar and other unhealthy foods even though only the youngest child has diabetes. If you visit their home, you won't be served candy or sweets of any kind. They simply don't think it is fair to ask one member of the family to eat a restricted diet while the rest of them indulge in whatever they wish.

Work sometimes demands difficult things of employees. My simple rule is to ask myself if this is something that I would be willing to do if the roles were reversed? I've found this to be a good acid test of whether I am being reasonable in my demands.

Chapter Nineteen: Advice for Leaders Assuming a New Role

"Change has a considerable psychological impact on the human mind. To the fearful it is threatening because it means that things may get worse. To the hopeful it is encouraging because things may get better. To the confident it is inspiring because the challenge exists to make things better."
- King Whitney Jr.

Whether you are going to a new company or just changing jobs in your existing company, people in new leadership roles face challenges. What you do in your first one hundred days will set the tone for your entire leadership assignment. It is important that you make a good first impression. And not just with your manager. You need to make a good first impression with co-workers, peers, and with your employees, as well.

I recommend you focus on the following five things to make sure you get off on the right foot:

1. Do A Quick Assessment. You need to know where your organization stands. Is it highly regarded for the positive impact they have on the business or is it lowly regarded for other reasons? The best way to determine this is to ask. Schedule one-on-one meetings with your employees, your internal customers, your key vendors, and your company's executives and ask for their candid assessment of what is being done right and what needs to be improved.

This will give you an idea of what needs to be changed and what should be left alone. It will also establish a rapport with your working colleagues that will pay dividends for years to come. Everyone appreciates being asked his or her opinion.

When I started my current job I knew that relationships between my department and our field operations were strained. I spent my first month on the job visiting our field operations people, traveling on airplanes and staying in hotels. I asked for their input and did a lot of listening. This really got me started on the right foot.

2. State Your Expectations Up-Front. Your new employees will be wondering how you operate. They will be anxious about how they should interact with you – their new leader. My advice is to tell people what they should expect right away. Take away the anxiety and tell everyone how you operate and what you expect, up-front.

Here are some of the things I tell my people when I take on a new leadership role:

- I will be on time for meetings. I will appreciate you being on time also.

- I don't expect you to work 60 hours a week. Don't expect me to work 60 hours a week either.

- I expect you to achieve a balance between work and family life.

- I expect you to ask for help if you are overloaded.

- I will try to minimize stress in your job. I believe that quality of life is an essential component of work. My grandmother always told me that contented cows give better milk. Please let me know if you are not contented.

- I don't expect you to come to me before you make a decision. You are empowered to do the great job you are capable of doing. If you need my help be sure to ask.

But don't think you need my permission before you act.

- I won't second-guess you.

- Take chances. Take risks. I will give you credit for all the good things you do, and I will take the blame for things that go wrong.

- Expect me to go directly to people who work for you for information. I will frequently circumvent the chain of command. Don't be alarmed or feel anxious; this is just my style.

If you have good leadership skills, telling people right away what they should expect from you and what you expect from them will relieve a lot of anxiety. If you do not have good leadership skills, communicating your expectations up front may create other anxieties, but at least people will know where they stand. Flip back to Chapter Four and review Jennifer's expectations. Note the difference between what Jennifer told people what to expect and what I tell people to expect.

Manage and Communicate Change. You are a new leader and your new organization is expecting change. And, change they will get. You are a big change from your predecessor just because you are not your predecessor. No doubt you will do things differently. Psychologists say that one of the top causes of stress is a change of manager. (Other top stress causes include a death in the family, the loss of a job, and a divorce.)

First, understand what causes employees anxiety. They fear organization change, changes in responsibility or authority, and the potential influx of new people – people the new leader may bring with him or her from their previous job. They fear changes in their work habits. They fear changes in the stature. Until you tell them differently, they will fear the worst. I offer the following advice:

Don't Shake Things up Unless It's Absolutely Necessary. I've known leaders who shake things up just to shake things up. I believe a new leader loses a lot of credibility when he or she begins to make changes when it's obvious they don't have a good grip of what's going on. Change for change's sake is not good. As soon as you determine that no change is needed – tell people. Don't let them waste time and energy worrying about when the hammer might fall.

If You Have to Shake Things Up Do It Quickly. You may discover that you don't have the very best people. You may discover that the organization's structure is unnecessarily bureaucratic and complicated. You may discover any one of a number of things that must be changed. Make your assessment quickly and get on with the necessary change. The sooner you make changes, the more quickly the organization can put it behind them and get on with business. Again, communicate your decision as soon as possible so people know where they stand.

Don't Bring *All* Your Former Cronies With You. The key word here is "all." It is OK for a new leader to bring some of their very best people along with them when they change leadership roles. If you determine you need new people, the best place for you to find new players is from your past. You know the people you've previously worked with. You know their strengths and weaknesses. And, they know you. My advice is – don't take this too far.

When BP acquired SOHIO in 1987, they replaced the top two executives in America with British executives. This was fine. But, the new BP executives also brought their secretaries with them. The company paid to relocate these secretaries from London, England, to the United States. This seemed a "little over the top" to most people.

I have known two new CFOs in my career that came into their new organization and replaced *all* their direct reports with people from their previous companies. This sent a clear message that these leaders believed that people from their former company were better than people in their new company. At one company where I worked, our new CFO came to us from ACME Corporation. After he had replaced all his direct reports with former cronies from ACME, the organization began to refer to his department as the ACME Finance group – not part of our company.

Accomplish Something. The best way to get off on the right foot is to accomplish something that will have a huge business impact. Hopefully it is something you can do quickly – to demonstrate that you and your organization will have a positive impact. Let me give you some examples:

As I said earlier, I spent the first month of my current job visiting field operations in twelve states asking them how my department could serve them better. I heard several clear, consistent messages about things that needed to be fixed. But the biggest thing I heard was that our systems weren't issuing daily work orders until 9:00 a.m. This meant that our service men and women, who started their workday at 7:30 a.m., were spending the first one and one-half hours waiting around for their work assignments. This definitely needed to be fixed. I took this back to my new organization and they met the challenge. In just a few weeks time, work orders were issued by 6:00 a.m. – well in advance of the start of the working day.

When I joined The Limited I discovered that my department was known for providing poor customer service. Computer departments exist to provide services to other parts of a business, and it is important that this service be good. It is important that the people in the department are customer service oriented. I began addressing this by first establishing a "customer service" organization. This group, which replaced an ineffective HELP Desk, became our first line contact with internal customers. We hand picked some of our best and brightest to staff this new group. Second, I met with my department and challenged them to begin thinking of others in the business as their customers. I told them that only two people in this world refer to their customers as "users," drug dealers and computer professionals. I asked them to start affording our internal customers the respect they deserved by calling them customers rather than users. Within weeks we began receiving compliments for our improved customer service.

In another job, I discovered that my predecessor didn't believe in technical training – in fact he didn't believe in any kind of training. His attitude, which he publicly stated, was that once people were trained, they used their newfound skills to leave the company and get a better paying job elsewhere. The truth was that people were leaving the company, in part, because they couldn't get trained on the latest and greatest technology. Furthermore, our department's computer technical skills were out of date and we were unable to deliver the best possible computer services.

Computer people value technical training. They want to be up on the latest computer hardware, the hottest operating system, the most popular programming languages, etc. Fortunately, it was budget preparation time, and from that day forward, our department had the money to provide the valuable technical training our people needed. It was only a few thousand dollars – less than 1% of my total budget. I remember being warned that my manager, the Chief Executive Officer, might challenge my budget addition. Sure enough she did, but not the way everyone expected. She said, "Les, the amount of money you have budgeted for training seems small. Please budget enough money so that our people can receive the best quality of training possible." Putting the money in the budget was a positive thing to accomplish. Having the CEO state publicly that she wanted my department to get the very best training available was icing on the cake.

Notice that none of these examples cost a lot of money or took a lot of time. Winning is contagious. Work for a quick, high-impact win and your entire organization will begin to perform at a higher level.

Don't Blame Your Predecessor. Some leaders arrive in their new job and immediately begin to blame their predecessor for everything that's wrong. Don't do this. Start with a clean slate. Take on challenges without affixing blame. Chances are that most others will know that you've inherited some problems – you don't need to constantly remind them. At any rate, you can only blame the past for a short period of time. After that, if you haven't fixed problems, they are rightfully yours.

In summary:

Make your *own* assessment of what's right and wrong about your new organization right away. Don't rely solely on the opinions of others.

Anticipate that the organization fears change. If you do need to change, get on with it. The sooner you replace key people, change organization structure, etc. the better.

Don't change for change's sake.

Your new organization is wondering what kind of person you are and how to interact with you. Don't make them figure this out as you go. Rather, lay down your working style and expectations up front.

It's OK to bring some of your very best people along with you from your previous job, but resist the temptation to make wholesale replacements with your cronies.

Don't blame your predecessor for things that are wrong. It's your organization now and any problems are now your problems. It's your job to fix them – not to affix past blame.

Finally, do something which will demonstrate the positive impact you can have – and do it quickly. Remember your first 100 days on the job will leave a lasting impression.

Chapter Twenty:
Develop Excellent Relationships with Strategic Business Partners

"Relationships of trust depend on our willingness to look not only to our own interests, but also the interests of others."
- Peter Farquharson

When I took my job as Senior Vice President & Chief Information Officer at a large specialty retailer, the first thing I did was read the information technology strategy that my predecessor had prepared. I found the following statement:

> Our strategy is to broaden the number of suppliers of information technology services to our company as much as possible. Our goal is to have several active suppliers for the same product or service, and to achieve the best possible pricing by constantly requiring them to compete against one another on a cost basis.

I was shocked. This was 180 degrees out of sync with my philosophy. My philosophy is to minimize the number of vendor/ suppliers we do business with and to look for strategic partnership relationships.

Most organizations have too many suppliers, even if they don't have a specific strategy of supplier proliferation like my predecessor at the specialty retailer mentioned above. Good leaders evaluate their list of suppliers and work to keep the number to a minimum. Great leaders look for ways to expand business with strategic business partners – not add new suppliers for new products and services. Every supplier takes time and costs money. Every supplier would like you to think they are strategic. Every supplier wants face time with the leader. The fewer the number of suppliers, the more efficient your operation.

Even after the supplier list has been paired down, you may still have thirty or more suppliers and not all of them will be "strategic." So the first step is to determine which vendors and suppliers are strategic. I define a strategic business partner as *a vendor or supplier who has the capability to significantly help my company achieve its goals and objectives.* I have never had a job (no matter how big) where more than 10 vendors and suppliers fit this description. In most of my jobs, the list was 5 or 6 companies long.

These are the people you will want to spend time with. These are the people you will want to forge a partnership relationship with. As for the others on the list – those that are not strategic – let someone else deal with them. You cannot afford to spend time with them all. As the leader, your time should be focused on those who can help your business the most.

Once I have determined that a vendor or supplier is strategic, I make sure they know they are strategic and why. I let them know which other vendors are on my strategic business partner list and why. I make sure they know they are one of a select few that I feel this way about. I make sure they know they are special and I am expecting more from them than just supplying a product or service.

From that point forward, I treat them like they are part of my business, as an extension of my staff. I communicate with them the same way I do with my direct reports, freely and openly. I share our business's goals, objectives, and strategies. I share my department's goals, objectives and strategies. I let them know what roadblocks we see in achieving these. The more they know about my organization, the better they can potentially help.

I tell them I would like to see them, face-to-face, at least once a quarter. I tell them if they need to see me more often, I will always make time for them. They are that important! I tell my assistant to book an appointment with me when they ask for one. No questions asked.

I don't just talk to them when there is a "problem." I call them when they have done something good – to compliment and thank them.

I return their phone calls and electronic mails promptly. I tell them I am looking for win-win opportunities. And, I don't beat them up. Many companies (retail is especially bad) treat their suppliers like dogs. They have this "I am the customer and you should do whatever I tell you to do" attitude. I don't treat any of my suppliers this way, but I am especially careful with my strategic business partners.

I tell them if they need a positive customer reference, I will provide it. If they need a quote from me for a magazine or newspaper article, I tell them I am willing. I let them know that just as they are willing to help me be successful, I am also willing to help them be successful.

I tell them I am willing to work with them as a "beta" test site for new products or services.

I build an executive level relationship with my strategic business partners. I get to know the boss's boss of the person who calls on my organization. This is the person who will be able to help me if I need something special.

Great leaders identify their strategic business partners and treat them well. Great leaders spend lots of time with strategic vendors and suppliers but don't spend time with non-strategic vendors and suppliers. Great leaders allow their strategic business partners to help them be more successful. Great leaders seize opportunities for win-win business relationships to keep the alliance strong.

Chapter Twenty-one: Take a Sincere Personal Interest in People

"If you would win a man to your cause, first show him that you are his sincere friend."
- Abraham Lincoln

"Hold faithfulness and sincerity as first principles."
- Confucius, The Confucian Analects

Caring, which is demonstrated by showing concern for others, is a huge asset for a leader. When you demonstrate sincere concern for the well being of other people it makes them feel worthwhile.

First, allow me to offer a word of caution before we proceed. This is *not* something you can fake! If you are not *genuinely* concerned about and interested in individuals, don't attempt to adopt this recommendation. Employees will see right through you.

Fortunately, caring and showing concern for other people is something that comes naturally for me. My parents raised me this way, and I couldn't change even if I wanted to. If you are also this type of person, here are some things you might want to consider:

Call Employees by Name. No matter how large your organization, you should know everyone's name. When you pass them in the hall, don't just say "Hi." Say "Hi Jim," with a big smile on your face. In one of my early leadership roles, I had nearly 500 men and women reporting to me. I made it a point to call each and every person by name. I admit that I had to carry a cheat sheet for several months, but I always called every person by name. These men and women told me later how much they appreciated it.

Know Something About Employees. For me, knowing a

person's name is not enough. I also like to know something about each person. Are they married or in a serious relationship? Do they play golf, tennis, softball, etc? Do they enjoy sports, the theatre, or traveling? Do they have children? And, on and on. Show an interest in their interests. Let them know you care. You should be able to carry on a conversation with people around their personal interests.

Be gracious when an employee asks you to do something that makes you uncomfortable. I am not a smoker. In fact, I have never put a cigarette in my mouth. But, as a young Air Force officer, I learned that when a young airman came to me and said, "Lieutenant, my wife just had a beautiful baby girl. Have a cigar," the correct response was to take the cigar, light it up on the spot, and say thank you. I disposed of the cigar as soon as the airman was out of sight, but, in his presence, I accepted his offer with appreciation and kindness.

Know Employees' Work. You should always know what employees are working on. They are doing the work for you – and for the betterment of the organization. It will mean a lot if you, the leader, acknowledge their work and tell them how much it is appreciated. You should also know when people are being overworked – and care enough to tell them.

I recall a time when my network group was attempting to upgrade all the personal computers and installing a new network operating system, at the same time. Frank, my Director of Networks, was working way too hard. Most of his work needed to be done at night when no one else was around, and oftentimes he worked the entire night through. Only to go home, catch a couple of hours of sleep, and then come in the next day to deal with more problems. I saw what Frank was doing and told him to stop! I told him it was OK to work a little bit of overtime, but I didn't want to see him working day and night for weeks on end.

He objected and told me that he needed to get the work done because he did not want to let the business down. I told him what he needed was more staff – not more hours of work. This was clearly a staffing issue. I threatened to fire him if I caught him working both day and night again.

Later Frank told me, "I really needed that stern lecture you gave me. You were right. I wasn't doing anyone any good by working those crazy hours. I really appreciate you bringing me back down to earth. I really respect you for recognizing that I was killing myself and letting me know it was OK to back off and wait for reinforcements." Frank and his family are still good friends today – ten years later.

Visit Inconvenient Locations. Some employees are easy and convenient to see and some are not. When I was stationed in Alaska, the 500 men and women who worked for me were scattered far and wide – literally all over the state. None of my employees were in the same building as my office. The closest group was about a quarter of a mile down the street, an easy walk. Others were several miles away. About one hundred were posted on different remote mountaintop sites around the state. I was able to visit those who were a few blocks and/or miles away on a weekly basis. Those in remote areas I visited less often. But, I saw everyone as frequently as I could, and I talked with him or her via phone between visits. It was important to me that everyone knew they were important and deserved some of my time. I believe it was also important to them.

Do a Lot of Walking Around. Unfortunately, if you wait for employees to come to you, you may wait a long time. The best way to stay in touch with employees is to walk around. I block time on my calendar for this. "Visit 1st Floor Data Center," for instance, is an entry on my calendar. The notion that people must come to you, the leader, if they want contact with you, is arrogant. Walk from desk to desk and let people know you care.

Great leaders:

- Let their people know they are important by knowing and caring about their personal well- being.
- Can call everyone in his or her organization by name.
- Know what people are working on.
- Visit their employees, no matter how far away or inconvenient that may be.

Chapter Twenty-two:
Focus on the Moment

"The only factor becoming scarce in a world of abundance is human attention."
- Kevin Kelly, in *Wired*

Have you ever had a conversation with someone and realized they were not really there? Have you ever sat in a meeting while thinking about a totally different topic? Have you ever noticed yourself thinking about your family at work, and thinking about your unfinished work when you're with your family? This is no way to lead your life, let alone to lead an organization.

Good leaders let people know that they are at the very heart of things, not at the periphery. Great leaders give their employees 100% of their attention when they are together. Great leaders make everyone feel that they make a difference and that gives their work meaning.

One of my leaders at British Petroleum was a habitual multi-tasker. I would go to his office for a scheduled meeting and our conversation would be constantly interrupted. He answered *every* telephone call. The phone would ring and he answered it in mid sentence, in spite of the fact that he had a secretary who could have picked up his calls during meetings. When he wasn't answering the telephone, he worked through his in-box, simultaneously trying to keep up with our discussion. Occasionally I would stop to ask him what he thought. It was frustrating when he said, "What? I'm sorry, what did you say?" If someone else walked up to the door, he would interrupt our meeting to ask what he or she wanted. Sometimes, he would stop our meeting and begin another meeting with them, on the spot. He treated everyone the same way he treated me. Everyone felt that we were not very important to him, and that what we were working on was also not very important to him. He was a good example of how to *not* focus on the moment.

In contrast, another of my leaders was the exact opposite. When he and I had a conversation, his focus was 100% on me. He did not allow distractions. His phone calls either rolled to voice mail or were picked up by his secretary. He closed his office door – a signal that he did not wish to be disturbed for any reason – a signal that what he was doing at that moment in time was the only thing that mattered. When I was with him, he made me feel like I was important. He made me feel like what I was working on was the most important thing in the world. This is how he made everyone feel. This is the kind of leader you should strive to be.

I have an open door policy. I tell everyone that if my door is closed, it means I do not want to be interrupted. But as long as my door is open, they should feel free to interrupt me. When someone walks through my open office door, I quit whatever I am doing and focus and concentrate on what they have to say. I make eye contact and engage myself in the conversation. I ask questions. I offer advice. As one of my former employees told me:

> One thing I believe I learned from you was that when someone is in my office I should give him or her my full attention. I shouldn't be looking at emails or picking up the phone when it rings. It goes a long way with the person you are talking to.

Hopefully employees know that, for the moment they are talking with me, they are my complete focus. Hopefully people know that what they came to talk to me about was important.

Living in the present moment can be a constant challenge, but it is an important leadership characteristic. Employees who are heard will feel more respected, more appreciated, and will be more productive. In business relationships, people will recognize your capabilities by your competence and practical people skills. Studies by Yale psychologist Robert Sternberg indicate that one of the most important traits of the "intelligent person" is people skills, which do not require a high IQ.

Great leaders:

   - Let people know they are important.

   - Focus and concentrate on what they are doing right now.

   - Give their employees 100% of their attention when they are together.

Chapter Twenty-three:
Beware of First Impressions

"If you would stand well with a great mind, leave him with a favorable impression of yourself; if with a little mind, leave him with a favorable impression of himself."
- Samuel Taylor Coleridge (1772 – 1834)

I've heard all my life that it is important to form a good first impression. My grandfather told me that when introduced to someone, I should always shake hands with a firm grip and make eye contact.

I know from first hand experience that a good first impression is very important when interviewing for a job. I've made some good first impressions on job interviews and I've made some bad ones, and believe me I knew the difference. Good first impressions are also important in other business relationships. Salesmen, for instance, are more successful if they make a good first impression. And, I maintain that a leader should also be concerned about making a good impression on his or her organization.

Research says that the following things can help make a good first impression:

Clothing and personal appearance
A professional attitude
A Smile
Maintaining eye contact
Concern for others

Listening as well as talking
Honesty
Humbleness/modesty
A firm handshake (I didn't see this one in the research,
but I think my grandfather was right.)
Body language
Verbal communications

All of these things are important. They can help make a good second, a good tenth, or a good one-hundredth impression as well.

I have come to accept the fact that others will form impressions about me based on the things listed above. I also know that for many individuals first impressions are lasting. Once they form an impression, it will be difficult or impossible to change. I've known leaders that were so confident they could "read" someone during a first meeting that they refused to even consider changing their mind later. I find this arrogant.

Don't be this kind of leader. Be careful not to lock in on the first impressions you form about others. Keep an open mind. I am human, and like everyone else, I walk away from every first encounter with an impression. And, most of the time my first impression proves to be right. I have pretty good instincts. But, there have been times when my first impression was not right. I was glad, on those occasions that I was willing to change my opinion as more information and experience was gained. I think you will be a better leader if you also take this approach.

Peter worked for me in the Air Force. The first time we met he did not strike me as an "A" player. He was nervous and jittery. He seemed overly cautious and political. He was hostile toward me, and we didn't even know one another. It was almost like he had made up his mind, even before meeting me, that he didn't like me much. My first impression was that Peter was going to give me nothing but trouble. I immediately began to think about how I might replace him with someone more compatible with my leadership style and expectations.

But then I stopped myself. Something was obviously wrong. So I did one of my favorite things – I confronted him right then and there. The conversation went something like this:

> Les: "Peter, although we've just met I sense that there is something about me that you don't particularly like. I'd like for you to give me a chance. Can you tell me what's bothering you? It won't go beyond these walls. It will be just between you and me."
>
> Peter: "I don't like officers. I especially don't like young Captains. I will do what you tell me to do. I will follow your orders. But don't expect me to like you. It ain't gonna happen."
>
> Les: "What have officers in general and young Captains in particular done to you to make you dislike us?"
>
> Peter: "I'd rather not say. It's personal."
>
> Les: "I understand. Carry on."

I could tell something was really bothering Peter but my judgment said that I shouldn't press it. A few weeks passed and Peter walked back into my office asking if he could talk to me.

> Peter: "I've thought about our first meeting and I've decided I behaved badly. I didn't treat you with the respect that an officer deserves."
>
> Les: "I believe respect must be earned not given just because I'm an officer. All I ask is that you give me an opportunity to earn your respect."
>
> Peter: "My wife divorced me last year to marry your predecessor, another young Captain. I've been bitter about it ever since, and I've been taking it out on every

officer I come in contact with. The past few weeks with you made me realize that Captains are not all alike. You are different. You seem to be a good guy."

Les: "Thank you. You seem to be a good guy too. Let's see if we can start again."

Peter turned out to be a great guy. He remarried while he was under my command, and his family and my family became close friends. In the end, I was very glad that I hadn't let my first impression govern our relationship.

Chapter Twenty-four: Smile (A Lot)

"What sunshine is to flowers, smiles are to humanity. These are but trifles, to be sure; but, scattered along life's pathway, the good they do is inconceivable."
Joseph Addison

"The most helpful quality in creating a positive first impression is a sincere smile. A smile communicates positive qualities. People perceive a genuine smile to portray a person who is sociable and likable."
- Unknown

A smile is an inexpensive way to improve your looks. My mother taught me to smile when I was in grade school. She told me to always have a smile on my face because a smile communicates friendship, kindness, happiness, and a positive outlook.

My mother said, "Smile and others will smile back." It's true. Try it. Smile at someone – there is a good chance they will smile back. Even if that someone is a perfect stranger, they will most likely smile right back.

When others describe me, they often describe me as the guy who is always smiling. One of my executive peers joked that he had never seen a computer guy who smiled as much as I do. He said I must have something devious in mind, because it just wasn't natural for a computer guy to smile all the time. He was joking. His joke made everyone else smile even more. Smiling is good!

If you don't smile naturally, try training yourself to smile more often. Once you've changed your psyche to a smiling one, it will be hard for you to go back. Here are some specific times when smiles are most important:

When the going gets tough. It is easy to smile when things are going great. You should also smile when things are not going well. A leader's smile during tough times can help improve an entire organization's attitude. A leader's smile sends the message that things aren't that bad, after all, which is usually the case.

When you greet someone. Whether walking down the street on a sunny afternoon or greeting someone who has come to your office for a meeting, a smile will go a long way to getting things off on the right foot. When Peggy showed up for our meeting yesterday, I smiled a big grin and said, "Hi Peggy, you're right on time."

When you meet someone. My grandfather always told me that a firm handshake and eye contact were important when meeting someone for the first time. A warm smile is just as important. It lets them know you are genuinely happy to make their acquaintance.

At the beginning of a presentation. Making a presentation to the higher ups can be stressful. Start your presentation with a smile and the tension will fade away.

At meetings. Important meetings will go better if you smile occasionally. Start the meeting with a smile and the atmosphere will be more fluid.

So smile a lot. Not only is it good for others, it is good for you. Psychologists tell us that people who smile are usually happier. Smiling sends a message to the brain – I'm happy.

Chapter Twenty-five:
Manage Time Effectively

"Never before have we had so little time in which to do so much."
- Franklin D. Roosevelt

I said earlier that no matter how much communication there is, employees never think it is enough. The same thing is true with time. No one ever thinks they have enough time. People say, "If only we had a just a few more hours in each day." My bet is that if they had a few more hours in each day, most of them would find ways to fill that up as well.

Great leaders know how to manage their time effectively. I am grateful for a time management class I took as a young Air Force officer. I still remember and practice what I learned in this class. I am also thankful that I worked my way through college. I worked 40-45 hours per week and carried a full college load for four years. I slept only a few hours a day. I had few precious hours left for studying and fun. The only way I was able to do all this was to manage my time very, very well.

I continue to manage my time well today. It is a fact that there is always much more to do than time to do it. Yet, I can count on one hand the times I've worked more than 50 hours in a week. Yet, I haven't missed a deadline. I rarely work on a weekend. And, I always have enough time.

The following tips can help you achieve this as well:

Don't Do Other's Jobs. I surround myself with the very best people and, having done so, I get out of the way and let them do their jobs. Not having to do their jobs frees my time up to do my own job better.

Don't Bite off More than You Can Chew. Remember, you will get more credit for doing a handful of things really, really well than for doing a lot of things poorly.

Resist the Temptation to be Involved in Everything. Some things are none of your business. Other things are under control without you being involved. I don't meddle in things that I know are on track.

Focus on Quality not Quantity. I focus on "what" I accomplish – not on how many things I get done or how many hours it takes me to do them. And, I encourage everyone in my organization to do the same. Individuals who judge others by the number of hours they work remind me of the college professor who graded term papers based on their weight, not their content. A friend of mine calls this the "thud factor."

Anticipate and Work Ahead. When I was working full time to pay my way through college, I asked my professors to tell me when they planned to schedule major assignments and exams several weeks in advance, so that I could prepare for these when I could grab a few spare minutes here and there. Given my very tight work/class schedule, I knew that if I waited until the week these things were due, I might not have enough time to get them done.

I do the same thing with my work. For instance, I review the Corporate Calendar to see there is a Board of Director's meeting in three weeks time. I know I will be asked to present my department's new five-year plan. Rather than wait for the Corporate Secretary to call me and ask me for something the week before the board meeting, I start working on my presentation now.

Block Time for Yourself. I schedule time on my calendar for *me* to do work. It is easy to find yourself in back-to-back meetings and conference calls. And, in this day of electronic calendars, others can check your availability and schedule you for meetings quite easily. At the end of the day you realize that you have been booked morning to night and still have your own work to do. Do yourself a favor and block some time each day for you to get your own work done. Don't compromise your time just because someone wants you to attend another meeting.

Come in Early. I come in before the official workday starts – before the phone starts ringing, the meetings and conference calls begin, and other people are around to "drop by." I find it is the best time to get things done. Note: If you are not an early bird, you can accomplish the same thing by staying a little later than others.

Handle Things Once. I "handle" a message or piece of correspondence one time and only one time, if possible. I know individuals who read through every message and piece of correspondence, and then they stick them into piles to deal with later. They must handle each of these again to take action. It is much more efficient to take action the first time through. And, remember that it's OK if that action is to throw it in the trash bin.

Approach Things Differently. Thousands of things come through my office every year. I classify them as either an A, B, C, or F items and deal with them as follows:

"A" items are things you must do immediately. A good example of an "A" item is something that comes from your manager. If you don't treat items from your manager with urgency and importance, you will have other problems. Another example is a query from a customer. Customers are the reason we are in business. When they ask for help, that request should be dealt with immediately. For me, a report or analysis that I requested from someone in my organization is also an "A" item. If someone has taken the time to prepare something I requested they deserve quick feedback from me.

"B" items are things you need to deal with, but not immediately. My presentation to the Board of Directors in three weeks time is a good example. These I put in a "to do" stack or drawer, and work on them when I get a few spare minutes.

"C" items are things that you aren't sure require your action. They sound important, but you just aren't sure. An "urgent" request from a co-worker for sales data could fall into this category. I put these items in my bottom desk drawer. If I receive the same request again in a few days, I retrieve the original item from my desk and take the necessary action. If, on the other hand, three months go by and I haven't received a follow-up request, I throw the original piece of correspondence away, making room for the next round of "C" items.

"F" items are things that you immediately know are a waste of time. These things are so worthless that I even skip the letters "D" and "E" to label them. And, there are a lot of them. I get 50 phone calls, 100 emails, and two-dozen pieces of mail every day. About 20% of this will help me be successful. I've learned to quickly filter through this myriad of "stuff" (a technical term), and dispense with the unnecessary without delay. I can usually tell if an email is important just by reading the title. I have caller ID so I can tell which phone calls need to be answered. I only spend meaningful time on those things that are important. I know this is hard for some individuals to do. They are afraid they might miss something if they skip reading an email and/or don't answer a phone call. My advice is to let it go. Learn to recognize "F" items quickly and then throw them into the trash bin without delay. You will be much more effective.

I recall the story about Dr. Scott Peck, a psychiatrist, and author of two best selling books. Oprah Winfrey was interviewing him on her afternoon television show in 1994.

Oprah: "Scott, you have written six or seven books, you tour the country giving lectures, you are presently writing a new book, you have a practice in Psychotherapy and you spend time with your family. How do you find the time to do all of this?"

Scott: "I spend two hours a day thinking about what is important in my life and what is not. I tell people I am praying so they won't interrupt. I do not spend any time on activities that are not important to my life. And, I don't watch your show."

This pretty much sums up my approach to time management. I spend time only on things that are important – and I don't watch the Oprah Winfrey show.

Chapter Twenty-six:
Be Customer Service Oriented

"Be everywhere, do everything, and never fail to astonish the customer."
- Macys Motto

"Your most unhappy customers are your greatest source of learning."
- Bill Gates, Business @ The Speed of Thought

Everyone has customers – people they provide a product or a service to. I worked in the retail business for nearly eight years. It was obvious that our customer was the person who shopped in our stores and hopefully purchased our merchandise. This was usually a woman (women even made the majority of purchases for our men's businesses such as Structure or Abercrombie & Fitch). We could identify our best customers – those who bought the most merchandise from us – and reward them with a frequent shopper program.

But, I was the Chief Information Officer. I ran the computer department. Perhaps less obvious was the fact that I had customers as well. My department provided computer services that allowed finance people to crunch the numbers. And we provided computer services that helped human resource associates with employee management and payroll. We also provided computer services that got merchandise in our stores and the computer services that drove the cash registers ringing sales. It was important that my internal customers received good service. It was important that my internal customers were happy and satisfied. My customers were the people working in finance, human resources, purchasing, distribution, and the people working in our stores. The better my department served them, the better we ultimately served our external customers – the men and women who bought merchandise in our stores.

When I arrived at one of my jobs, I quickly realized that my department was definitely *not* customer service oriented. My first clue came when my personal computer broke and I called the "help desk." The telephone extension for the help desk was 4-3-5-7. This spelled H-E-L-P on the telephone dial pad. This made the number easy to remember – very clever.

The conversation went like this:

Help Desk: "Help Desk here."

Les: "My personal computer is broken. I am getting an error message."

Help Desk: "What is your name, your telephone number, and where do you work?"

Les: "My name is Les Duncan, my phone number is 4441, and I work in the computer department."

Help Desk: "OK. I'll have someone call you back."

Les: "But wait a minute. You're the help desk. Can't you help me?"

Help Desk: "No, I'm the computer room operator. I have a full time job keeping the mainframe computers operating. They told me to answer this Help Desk line when it rings. I don't know much about personal computers."

Les: "How many people have called you this week and how many people have you been able to help?"

Help Desk: "I've received hundreds of calls this week, but I'm not actually supposed to provide any help. My job is to take your name and phone number and then pass it along to someone else who might be able to help."

Les: "How long will this take?"

Help Desk: "I don't know. I just take down the information and pass it along."

Wow! This was frustrating. I called my computer Help Desk and got no *help*. The guy who took my call not only didn't know how to solve my problem, he believed it wasn't his job. And, if he treated me this way, who knows how he treated others? I was his department head.

I knew this had to change and change fast! I selected a few of my best and brightest people – people who knew a lot about personal computers – and asked them to form a new group which we called "Customer Service." The words "help desk" were gone forever. We changed the telephone extension. Like me, others had learned that you got no help from the help desk. It had even been renamed the "Helpless Desk." Changing the telephone extension and name of the group sent the message that this was a new group of people – not the old help desk.

We brought in professionals to train our new customer service team on how to be customer service oriented and on how to deal with the occasional irate caller. I felt the new group was so important that I had it report directly into me. Our objective was to solve 90% of all problems on the first phone call and we succeeded.

Next, I asked my group to help change our department's image to one of customer service. I reminded them that we existed to provide computer services to the rest of the business. I told them that we were currently not regarded as a service oriented organization. I asked them to stop referring to our customers as "users."

"There are only two people in this world who refer to their customers as users – drug dealers and computer professionals. From this day forward I'd like you to help me afford our internal customers the respect they deserve and refer to them as customers – not users."

It is amazing how individuals will respond when you ask them to help. The word "user" disappeared from our vocabulary, the computer department became obsessed with customer satisfaction, and when people called our customer service number, they got help.

In the retail business, Nordstrom is famous for its customer service. They reward their employees for outstanding customer service, and some of the tales are legendary. Nordstrom believes, for instance, that a customer should not be disappointed when they come to their store. They believe that a customer who comes to their store expecting to buy a pair of shoes and not finding what they want constitutes a disappointing shopping experience.

Legend says that a customer went to a store to buy a new suit. When it came time to purchase a matching pair of shoes, the customer didn't fine anything that they liked. The sales clerk believed he knew what the customer wanted – he also knew Nordstrom didn't stock it. He excused himself to run down the block to another department store, where he purchased several pairs of shoes in the customer's size. Upon his return, the customer was delighted. The customer purchased one of the four pairs of shoes not knowing they were from the other department store and left happy. There are a million of these legends about Nordstrom. Stories about sales clerks jumping through hoops to make customers happy. We should all strive for happy customers. We should all try to turn our customers into our strongest supporters.

When I returned from London to the United States to head up BP America's computer department, I inherited a *corporate* department that was also in need of change. I use the word *corporate* here on purpose. In many companies *corporate* is associated with large, centralized, bureaucratic, arrogant organizations of the past. That certainly described the corporate computer department at BP America in the early 1990s.

Again, I called my team together and asked for their help. I told them we needed to transform the organization from one that was loathed to one that was revered for its outstanding customer service. We adopted the slogan: "Our job isn't finished until the customer is satisfied." And we did our best to live up to it.

We decided that we would subject our service to the acid test. We told our internal customers that if they could find better/lower cost services than ours outside the company from someone like EDS or IBM, they were free to go. This meant that we would have to reduce the size and cost of our internal organization accordingly. If all our internal customers went elsewhere, our internal organization would cease to exist. We would be out of jobs. This was a little scary – but it demonstrated that we were serious about providing outstanding customer service. In the end we only lost one internal customer to an outside source, and this was someone that had so many bad experiences with the corporate computer department in the past that they just couldn't get past it.

We offered our internal customers at BP America the opportunity to get their computer services from someone else so we could know how satisfied they were with our services. In hindsight, we could have accomplished the same thing much less radically. If you want to know if your customers are satisfied – just ask them.

You can ask them directly, during a conversation. Communication with your customer is a good thing. But, perhaps the best way to ask them is via a formal customer satisfaction survey.

Customer Satisfaction Surveys:

Surveying my customers to determine their level of satisfaction is something I have done for a dozen years now. It is the best feedback my organization and I can receive. I try to do this annually so we can tell whether our service is improving or declining. I make the responses anonymous so that people can freely say what they need to say.

First I ask people to rate their level of satisfaction by organization entity. The question usually reads something like this:

On a scale of 1-5, how satisfied are you with the quality and timeliness of the service you receive from the _____ team?

I repeat this question for each sub-group in my organization. Next I ask them how satisfied they are with specific new initiatives that have been implemented over the past year. For instance, we may have installed a new computer application to support sales. I simply ask them how satisfied they are with that new application.

I invite them to provide both constructive and appreciative comments about individual departments and initiatives. I ask them not to make their comments personal. If they have a specific axe to grind with an individual, I encourage them to contact that person and talk with them directly.

Then I ask them a series of questions, the answers to which usually provide specific, valuable feedback:

Name three things we do exceptionally well.

Name three things we most need to improve.

Name one person who has provided exceptional customer service over the past year.

Overall, what grade would you give us? A, B, C, D, or F.

The numerical satisfaction ratings by department provide useful feedback; however, it has been my experience that the most valuable feedback comes from the four questions directly above.

Most organizations can and will work to improve three things. And, my experience is that three things listed as areas for improvement in this year's survey can easily be listed as things you do well in later years. Singling out specific people who have provided exceptional customer service is great. As the leader, you can take great pleasure in telling these people how highly their service is regarded. Finally, the grade is the bottom line. Are we an "A" organization or do we fail in the eyes of our customers and get an "F"?

Great leaders recognize the value of good customer service. Great leaders understand that good customer service is just as important for internal customers as it is for external customers. Great leaders ask their customers how they are doing and take actions to keep doing what they are doing well and to improve those areas that need improvement.

Chapter Twenty-seven:
Set a Good Example

"Live in such a way that you would not be ashamed to sell your parrot to the town gossip."
- Will Rogers

"People are changed, not by coercion or intimidation, but by example."
- Unknown

Great leaders know that others are looking to them for example. Great leaders understand that everything they say and do can have an impact on the organization. The best leaders realize that example is not the main thing in influencing others – it is the only thing.

In the military, *not* providing a good example can lead to a court martial. Written into the military laws is something called "conduct unbecoming." Translated, this means that it is against military law for an officer or enlisted person to behave in a way that disgraces his country, his organization, his rank or his uniform. This law applies to military people *even* when they are off duty. Under the law, you can be court-martialed for such things as driving under the influence, adultery, being drunk in public, or even starting a fistfight. The message is loud and clear. Behave yourself – both on and off duty.

Sometimes I think there should be a "conduct unbecoming" law for leaders. I've seen leaders work hard to earn respect from their employees only to lose it by behaving badly. Think about it. How much respect do you have for your leader when you know he or she steals? Or when they lie? How about when they just plain behave badly? Let me give you a few examples from my work experience.

Jim was a department head with twenty years service with our company. He had risen from an entry-level position to become a Vice President. Not everyone liked Jim, but most everyone respected him for his business knowledge and technical skills. Then, one Friday evening, Jim went out with some colleagues from work and had too much to drink. His behavior was embarrassing, to say the least, and his co-workers tried repeatedly to get him to stop drinking – but he didn't. Eventually, when he was ready to go home, he refused to allow anyone to drive him. He insisted that he was able to drive himself. The next morning, the local paper reported that Jim had been arrested for driving under the influence. According to the newspaper report, this was Jim's third DUI offense.

On the following Monday, Jim's escapades and arrest were the talk of the organization. Some recalled his rambunctious behavior and how embarrassed they had been for him and themselves. Others talked about the poor judgment he exercised by not allowing someone to drive him home. Others were astounded that this was his third DUI offense.

Robert was also a department head. He had a reputation for being a family man, devoted to his wife and children. He proudly displayed family photographs in his office, and there were crayon drawings from his daughter pasted on his office walls.

One of the young men in Robert's department was getting married and several of his co-workers threw him a bachelor party. Robert wasn't invited – nor should he have been. Eventually, the young men wound up at a topless bar. These guys didn't normally go to topless bars, but this was a special occasion. About a half-hour after they arrived, they spotted Robert sitting, by himself, at a table across the building. At first they couldn't believe their eyes. Robert was a family man – this couldn't be him. But it was. Moreover, the girls obviously knew him – he was a regular.

Dan led a group of information technology professionals, and had a well-deserved reputation of stretching the truth. Once Dan told us a story about his move from San Francisco to Houston. According to

Dan, the moving company loaded all of his belongings onto a moving van, but tied his extension ladder to the undercarriage. When the truck arrived in Houston, they unloaded everything. Or so he thought. Almost as soon as the driver left the house, Dan discovered the movers had forgotten the extension ladder. Dan called the company and made arrangements for them to deliver the ladder at a later date.

The very next week the same driver with the same truck showed up at Dan's house, thanking him profusely. He explained that during the intervening week, his house had caught on fire, and he had used Dan's extension ladder to rescue his wife, three children and the family pets from their upstairs bedrooms, saving them from certain death. You see the driver didn't own an extension ladder. If Dan's ladder had not been inadvertently left on his truck, his entire family would have perished.

Dan had a million of these tall tales. Some of them might have been true. The problem was that you knew most of them were too grandiose to have ever happened, so you tended to not believe anything he said.

What a leader says and does on and off the job will affect how those he or she leads behaves, as well. Entire organizations can take on the personality of the leader. For instance, Microsoft is known for being innovative and competitive, a direct reflection of its founder and Chairman, Bill Gates. Wal-Mart's culture of being customer focused and frugal comes straight from Sam Walton, its founder.

The message here is act like you want people in your organization to act. If you want people to be customer oriented, you must be customer oriented. If you want people to be honest, you must be honest. If you want people to work hard and care about the results of their labors, then you should work hard and you should care about the results of your labors. It is important for leaders to behave the way they want others in their organization to behave.

Warren Deakins, President and CEO of Fidelity Mutual Life Insurance Company said it like this:

I believe it is unnatural for you to come in late and for your people to come in early. I think it is unnatural for you to be dishonest and your people to be honest. I think it is unnatural for you to not handle your finances well and then expect your people to handle theirs well. In all these simple things, I think you have to set the standard.

Evaluate your leadership behavior by answering the following questions:

- Do you whine, gossip or spread rumors?
- Are you supportive of your peers and co-workers, or are you critical?
- Do you neglect your family for work?
- Do you approach things in a direct and straightforward manner, or do you play politics?
- Are you defensive?
- Do you admit your mistakes, or do you make excuses or try to hide them?
- Are you honest?
- Are you reliable – even predictable?
- Do you work hard, but don't overwork?
- Do you give credit where credit is due?

It is possible for a leader to behave in all the right ways and still some people in his or her organization will behave badly. But, I believe that more people will behave badly if their leader sets the wrong example. And, if people are merely mocking the leader's behavior, it's pretty hard for the leader to say they are wrong.

This is another case where leading is like being a good parent. For instance, it's difficult for a parent to tell a child not to smoke or to criticize them if they do smoke, if the parent is a chain smoker. Do as I say, not as I do doesn't fly when raising children. It doesn't fly for leaders either.

I believe leaders (and everyone else) should live their lives as if they worked in offices with glass walls and everything they say is broadcast over a public address system. Train yourself to behave properly, even if you are alone, and you will be more likely to behave properly in public. And, don't say anything in confidence that you are not willing to have repeated – because there is a good chance that someone will repeat it.

Not only should the leader behave well, but his or her executive assistant should also behave well. The executive assistant is a leader's interface to the world. Others will ask his or her advice about dealing with you. Others will pump him or her for information – hoping to pick up a tidbit for the rumor mill. Many people fail to distinguish between the leader and the assistant. Every leader needs to hire an assistant that will emulate his or her personal and professional values.

I recall my early days at The Limited. I inherited a great executive assistant, who unfortunately left the company shortly after my arrival to stay home full-time with her new baby boy. A lower level secretary, June, in another department was about to lose her job because of cutbacks. June came to me and pleaded that I give her my assistant's job. She was distraught. I knew she wasn't capable of representing me well. I knew she didn't emulate my personal and professional values. But, I felt sorry for her and gave her the job.

June turned out to be even worse than I thought. She lacked the basic skills and abilities to do her job, and the other executive assistants didn't respect or accept her. Things were not going well for her.

Eventually, I sought advice from our Executive Vice President of Human Resources. He didn't pull any punches. He said, "Les, how June does her job, how she acts, and the way she dresses is a direct reflection on you. You need to hire an assistant that can represent you for the person you are." He was right – and I did.

Business lunches or dinners are good places to communicate good values. My personal policy is that the senior person at the table should pick up the bill. Many leaders don't do this. I have seen leaders intentionally pass a dinner bill to a subordinate. This way they can sign/approve the subordinate's expense report, and they don't have to send it to their manager for approval. This sends the wrong messages. It implies that the manager wouldn't approve. Well, if the manager wouldn't approve, why are you doing it? It also sends the message that the leader is trying to hide something – not being up front. Not being up front is a bad leadership characteristic. When the most senior person at the table pays the bill it sends the exact opposite message. It says that that person is confident that his or her manager supports what is going on and they aren't afraid to allow them to review and approve the expense.

Setting a positive example is a powerful leadership tool. Others will respect you for doing the right things. Others will emulate your good behavior. Your positive example can transform an entire organization into a better group of people. Unfortunately, the opposite is also true. Your bad behavior can turn an entire organization ugly. Everyone I know who knew the top executives at Enron and WorldCom were not surprised to learn of the fraud and accounting irregularities that were uncovered there. They had observed, firsthand, that these were not good people. They had observed, firsthand, that these guys and gals behaved badly.

Remember a leader's actions speak louder than words. Be a role model – set a good example. Your organization will follow.

Chapter Twenty-eight:
Celebrate Successes

Most people work hard. Organizations can get in the mode of cranking things out one right after another. You just finish one task and you're onto another one. Someone reaches an important milestone on the job or in life and it's hardly noticed. My advice is to stop occasionally and take time to celebrate.

The Limited did a great job of celebrating successes. Let me give you two examples:

We sold merchandise in hundreds of stores located in almost every shopping mall in the country. Each of our stores was staffed with an energetic and enthusiastic team of young women, led by a store manager. Store managers had difficult jobs. They worked at least six days a week, ten to twelve hours a day, including every weekend and holiday. They dealt with personnel issues, dissatisfied customers, out-of-stock issues – you name it, they did it. How they performed had a direct impact on the overall performance of our business. A good store manager could easily add ten to twenty percent to their store's sales and profit.

At the beginning of each year, store managers were given sales targets. At the end of each year the executive team celebrated those managers who performed the best (relative to their sales targets) by taking them to a five-star resort for three days of fun and relaxation – all expenses paid. We called this "President's Club."

This was a huge deal for our store managers. It was something they looked forward to all year long. A trip to President's Club was something they worked extra hard to earn. We provided lots of good food and drink, a costume night, games, parties, and unique activities like hot air ballooning and attending a polo match. Most store managers hadn't been to a five-star resort, let alone ridden in a hot air balloon or attended a polo match. It was unbelievably expensive, but these store managers had earned it. The three days were capped off with a formal ceremony. Each manager was called onto a stage, individually, to receive a plaque and a personal congratulation from our President and CEO. And, after it was all over, each person received a video of the three-day event, in which they were the stars. It was a great way to celebrate their success.

The second example involves promotions. In other companies I've worked for, the person being promoted is called into the manager's office and is told of their good fortune. Sometime later, the promotion is announced to others via a memo. Not at The Limited. At The Limited, promotions were an opportunity to celebrate. Allow me to describe "promotion day" at The Limited:

As people arrived for work they were told that there would be "announcements in the atrium" at 9:00 a.m. Excitement and positive energy began to build because everyone knew that this meant promotions were going to be announced. At the appointed time, every meeting, every telephone conversation, every bit of work stopped, and the entire company went to the atrium where department heads would take turns announcing promotions for their groups. The person being promoted had not been told in advance – it was a complete surprise – which made the celebration even more exciting. The entire company learned of and celebrated their promotion with applause, screams of joy, and sometimes a few tears. It was a grand celebration.

These are just two examples of how The Limited celebrated

successes. I could go on and on. One of the guys who worked for me at The Limited recently told me:

> I remember our monthly meetings where we always celebrated birthdays and anniversaries with cake and much fanfare.

Suffice it to say The Limited did a better job of celebrating personal and business successes than any other company I know of. It was something that was built into their culture and they were very good at it.

All birthdays are important. But, be sure not to allow someone to turn 21, 30, 40, 50, etc. without acknowledging them. Anniversaries are important, especially the 5-year, 10-year, 25-year and 50-year anniversaries. If you have taken a sincere interest in your employees you will know when these major milestones occur. If not, find someone else in your organization that is willing to do this for you, so that everyone can celebrate.

For every employee who works their butt off to accomplish something great at work, there is often a spouse, girlfriend/boyfriend, children, and others who made sacrifices back at home. Without the support and encouragement from these people, the employee would not have been so successful. That's why I believe in including families and close friends in celebrations as often as possible. Let me give you a few examples:

> At one of my jobs, one hundred fifty people worked extremely hard for two straight years to implement a new software package – one that transformed the way we did business. We had achieved several major milestones along the way, and we stopped to celebrate each of them. But, when the job was finally done, a

grand celebration was warranted. We rented the ballroom at a major hotel and celebrated our success, with our spouses, over a five-course surf and turf dinner. Dinner for three hundred – what a grand celebration! I gave a speech at the conclusion of the evening, which included a lot of humor, but most importantly, included a special thank you to all the families for the sacrifices they had made while we were working hard.

My wife and I open our homes to my employees and their families each year during the Christmas/ Hanukkah season. My wife decorates every room in the house with neat stuff we have acquired over our 35 years of marriage, from locations all over the world. The place is a showcase when she's finished. The invitation always says, "Parents are not permitted to attend without their children." One year we had 200 guests – nearly half of them were children under the age of ten. It's great fun and it is definitely a family event.

These days it's hard to find an employee who's been with the same company for more than a few years. That's why it's so important to celebrate when someone achieves five, ten, fifteen, or more years of service. At Atmos Energy, we celebrate these employees with a formal dinner at a fine restaurant. Husbands and wives are always included. The employee and their family get a great dinner out, a gift, and public recognition for their accomplishment.

There are thousands of ways to celebrate successes – and many of them don't cost a lot of money. You can celebrate a success by standing up in a department meeting and acknowledging your appreciation for someone's accomplishments. At British Petroleum, we rewarded outstanding performance with one month of free parking in our parking garage: a thirty-dollar prize. But, that thirty-dollar prize was highly valued, especially during the cold, Cleveland, Ohio, winter months. I like to celebrate successes by sending a personal, handwritten thank you note when someone does something great. We recently completed a new software installation on time, on budget, and with great benefit to the business. I sent a personal thank you to each of the 75 people who helped make this a success.

So, don't let life run away from you. Everyone is busy. Everyone is working hard. But it's important to stop occasionally, just for a moment, and celebrate success. Don't let a birthday, anniversary, or major accomplishment on the job go by without celebrating. And, be sure to acknowledge the important role that spouses, children, and friends play in your organization's success.

Chapter Twenty-nine:
Take Blame – Not Credit

"A real leader faces the music, even when he doesn't like the tune."
- Unknown

"To err is human, to blame the next guy even more so."
- Unknown

Great leaders pull up blame and push down credit. Insecure leaders grab credit and deflect blame.

As discussed in previous chapters, the best leaders provide tons of positive reinforcement to the people in their organization. They tell them when they have done a good job. They tell their boss and everyone else when someone has done an exceptionally good job.

But great leaders do more than this. They make sure that the people who do the good job get *all* the credit. And, when something doesn't go exactly as planned, they – not their organization – take the blame.

I can't help but recall the following story about a conversation between Brad and his boss, Mr. Jones:

Mr. Jones: "Brad, I just called to see how *you* are coming on those financial reports – the ones that *you* told me are going to be late this month."

Brad: "Those reports are finished, Mr. Jones."

Mr. Jones: "Finished?"

Brad: "Yes. I hired a new person, Pete. Pete did

them in no time. And, he did the sales forecast as well."

Mr. Jones: "Well the Chief Financial Officer will be very pleased when *I* tell him that *we* hired Pete and that *we* have completed all the reports ahead of schedule."

Brad: "I already told the Chief Financial Officer."

Mr. Jones: "You told the Chief Financial Officer?"

Brad: "Yes, he called me yesterday."

Mr. Jones: "The Chief Financial Officer called you?"

Notice that at the beginning of the conversation, when Mr. Jones thought the reports were going to be late, it was Brad's problem. But, as soon as Brad told him that Pete had completed the reports early, Jones tried to grab the credit. Jones would tell the Chief Financial Officer about the good job they had done.

In one of my leadership roles, I had about 200 people in my organization and was responsible for a $50 million annual budget. The budget was large enough that I had a full-time budget manager working directly for me. His only job was to monitor and control our department's expenses. My manager controlled a $600 million budget (including my $50 million) and he also had a full-time budget manager, who did nothing but watch over the money being spent. We paid both of these budget managers a good wage to make sure our expenses stayed in line. We met with them on a regular basis to make sure things were OK.

A one million-dollar accounting mistake was made. Six months passed before we discovered the error. I told my manager, and he was not happy. "A million dollars is a lot of money," he said. "How could you miss a million dollars?" My first reaction was to be defensive. I thought about all the weekly/monthly budget reviews that he and I had both sat through. His budget manager and my budget manager had assured us that things were on track. They had presented detailed financial reports to back up their statements.

But I realized that I was ultimately responsible and I took the blame. Then I set about finding out why the mistake had happened and figuring out ways to make sure it didn't happen again.

Even great leaders make mistakes. And organizations led by great leaders also make mistakes. My experience is that it's best to admit them. Tell your manager you've screwed up before he or she hears it from someone else. Then tell him what you are doing to make sure it doesn't happen again. Take the fall for your people.

I worked my way through college doing a variety of blue-collar jobs. One of these jobs was working on an assembly line making Coleman camp stoves. I was one of two "college kids" working the night shift. Ron Smith, one of the other college guys, was a brilliant young man with great potential.

One day during lunch break, Ron and I discussed our plans after graduating. We both had dreams of becoming successful business people. Ron made the following statement, which I will never forget:

> The key to getting ahead in the business world is to make sure your boss always knows when you have done something good, and just as importantly, make sure your boss knows when one of your peers does something wrong.

It still sends chills down my spine to recall than Ron believed this. Ron wasn't exactly my kind of guy, so I didn't bother to keep up with him after graduation, but my guess is that, with a philosophy like this, he didn't go very far.

Unfortunately, Ron isn't the only person I've encountered with this philosophy. I have worked in organizations where Ron's approach was practiced. However, I am grateful to Ron for teaching me a valuable lesson about how a leader shouldn't behave. Leaders who try to grab credit are usually not highly regarded – by their employees, their peers, or their superiors. Leaders who attempt to deflect blame and/or follow Ron's advice and try to spotlight the faults of others are even less highly regarded.

As Jim Collins says in his book *Good to Great*:

> Leaders look out the window to apportion credit to factors outside themselves when things go well (and if they cannot find a specific person or event to give credit to, they credit good luck). At the same time, they look in the mirror to apportion responsibility, never blaming bad luck when things go poorly.

You will automatically get credit when your organization excels – this will come without you trying to grab the credit from someone else. People are more likely to excel if they know they will receive the credit. People are also more likely to be bold if they know they won't get blamed for the occasional failure.

Chapter Thirty:
Market Your Organization

"In the modern world of business, it is useless to be a creative original thinker unless you can also sell what you create. People cannot be expected to recognize a good idea unless it is presented to them by a good salesman."
- David M. Ogilvy

The best leaders are also great public relations people for their organizations. Great leaders sing the praises of their people and the great things they do for their business. The very best leaders aren't shy about reminding others of their group's accomplishments.

Sometimes busy businessmen and businesswomen are not aware of what your organization has accomplished. In other cases they suffer from "corporate amnesia." They once knew that your team had done a great job, but they have since forgotten. It's almost like they are saying, "What have you done for me lately?" I know this might sound disrespectful or critical – but believe me, it is not. It is just a fact. That is why it is important that you, the leader, seize opportunities to remind others what your team has accomplished.

There is a fine line to walk here. On the one hand, you want to make sure that your team gets full credit for the good work they do. On the other hand, you don't want to be perceived as someone who is tooting his or her own horn. There are ways to manage this.

1. Give credit where credit is due – to the good people in your organization that did the work. Don't try to grab the credit for yourself. After all, they are the ones who deserve all the credit. Name names. It's much more palatable to blow your employees' horn than to blow your own horn.

2. Stick to the facts. Talk about what the people in your group have done in a simple, straightforward, factual manner. It is hard for someone else to take issue with the facts.

3. Share the Credit. Rarely is one person or one organization responsible for something good that happens. The message you should deliver is that your team has accomplished something good with the help of other people from other organizations.

There should be no shortage of opportunities for you, the leader, to market your organization. Yet, you don't want to over do it. So pick your spots.

One opportunity you won't want to miss is when you ask for money. For instance, every organization goes through an annual or semi-annual budget preparation process. There is never enough money to do everything that your organization wants to do and you will be competing for funds, along with others. Before you ask for dollars, remind your management of the things you have done for them recently. If you've done your job, it will reinforce the fact that the money allocated to your organization is money well spent.

Another opportunity you don't want to miss is when you talk with your customers – internal or external. I talk about the need for leaders to "hit the road" in a later chapter. This is all about being visible to your customers, suppliers, employees, and shareholders. When you visit your customers, be sure to tell them what you have already done. I have never met a customer who didn't want more. But, if they are reminded of the good things you've done for them in the past, they can be less demanding. You will also want to ask them what else you can do for them – how you can be even better.

Another good way to market your organization – to tell others about their great accomplishments – is to produce an annual report. Hopefully you set goals and objectives for your organization at the beginning of each year. If you don't you should start. Once you have established key objectives for your team, communicate them to senior management. At the end of the year, write a short (two pages or less) summary of how you did on each of these objectives. Not only is this good marketing, it also demonstrates that you do what you said you would do.

So far, I have addressed the need to market your organization internally. Don't underestimate the importance of also marketing your organization externally. When Federal Express developed their electronic tracking system, their President nominated the company for the Malcom Baldridge National Quality Award. They won the award.

I recently nominated my organization for CIO Magazine's Top 100 award, and we were selected as one of the most resourceful information technology organizations in the country. Receiving these types of prestigious, well deserved awards are a real morale boost to people and organizations. It reinforces the fact that they are doing really good work!

As a leader, you are in a unique position to nominate your organization for these awards. You won't be selected unless your team's accomplishments are worthy. But, even if you don't win the award, your organization will feel good that you thought them worthy of nomination.

The best leaders are front men and women for their organization. They remind others of the great things their employees have done. They do this internally, but they also seize opportunities to market externally. They understand that their entire organization gets a huge morale boost when they receive well deserved recognition for their accomplishments. In short, great leaders are their organization's biggest cheerleaders. But they don't over do it.

Chapter Thirty-one:
Identify Risks and Mitigate Them

"If we don't succeed, we run the risk of failure."
- Dan Quayle

We face risks in everything we do. The question is, do we allow ourselves to be consumed by these risks and paralyzed into inaction, or do we identify the risks, take steps to mitigate them and proceed?

Let's say you are sitting at home one morning and you decide to go to the grocery store to buy some milk. You grab your car keys, but then it hits you. There are risks involved. What if the car breaks down? What if you are involved in an automobile accident on the way there or the way home? What if the store has run out of milk? What do you do?

You might decide that it's just not worth the effort to buy milk. You might ask you neighbor to pick up your milk on his or her next trip to the store – thus transferring the risks to them.

But, most of us would just go to the store and buy milk. Most of us keep our car tuned and in good working order so it is unlikely to break down. Most of us drive carefully to avoid accidents. And most of us shop at stores that are well stocked. Most of us take steps to mitigate risks so we can carry on with our normal every day life.

Granted, this sounds a little silly. But, the same kind of thing applies to the workplace. Let me give you an example.

After spending three months evaluating multi-million dollar software packages, we had narrowed it down to two potential suppliers. Both provided excellent products. We listed the pros and cons of each vendor's software and decided that one vendor's product was a better match for our requirements.

Throughout the evaluation process my manager kept asking about risks. He had heard about other companies who had spent two or three times their original budgets to install new software. He knew, firsthand, about companies whose business had been badly disrupted by a poor software installation. What if these things happened to us? My response was, "There are a number of significant risks involved with this new software, but I believe there is no risk that can't be mitigated. Let me show you how we are addressing this."

The following is what I presented to my manager:

Potential Risk	Mitigation
Underestimating the time and resources needed to complete the project could cause total implementation costs to be double or triple the budget	Negotiate a risk sharing contract with business partners with financial incentives to them to complete the project under budget and financial penalties if the project is completed late Implement a 24-Hour decision rule to keep the implementation process from bogging down – no decision could take more than 24 hours to make
Underestimating the amount of computer hardware required could result in an additional multi-million dollar budget over run	Negotiate a fixed price contract with the computer hardware vendor in exchange for agreeing to serve as an R&D site for emerging technology and providing a positive customer reference should their new technology prove to work well

Experienced, key consultants may be moved to another company's project	Include contractual guarantees that key consultants would remain on the project for the duration
Employees may take their new found skills and leave for more money at another company	Provide retention bonuses and stock options to retain key employees
Business Disruption	Conduct three end-to-end tests prior to implementation Schedule the implementation for a non-peak business period
Inability to make needed software changes in a timely manner	Insist that programmers from the software vendor be located on-site and be part of the project team
Post implementation costs could rise due to the need to purchase additional software licenses as the company grows	Negotiate a software contract which allows our business to grow for three years after implementation at no additional cost

I told my manager that these were all deal breakers. If we couldn't get retention bonuses, negotiate the right contracts, and get access to the right people, we would back away from the deal.

My manager was the nervous type, so he continued to worry about these things, even after I shared this mitigation strategy with him. But, in the end, my approach paid off. Yes, we didn't have enough computer hardware, but our hardware vendor honored their commitment and provided more hardware at no additional cost, saving us millions of dollars. Putting the software in took longer than expected, but our consultants and contractors stayed with us through the extra months and graciously accepted their late penalties. Key employees stayed with us, also, to collect their bonuses and stock. By identifying the risks of implementing new software up-front and proactively developing a strategy to mitigate them we were successful.

It's always easier to find reasons for not taking a risk than to find ways to mitigate them. Great leaders don't shy away from challenges just because there may be risks. Great leaders find ways to mitigate the risks and get the job done.

Chapter Thirty-two: Gather Information from the Source

An alternative title for this chapter might have been, "Ignore the Chain of Command."

Traditionally, if the president of a company wants to know how a new marketing initiative is going, he asks the senior vice president of sales and marketing who then asks the director of marketing. The director of marketing goes to the product development manager who asks his or her marketing analyst – the person who actually knows the answer to the president's question. The same process is then followed in reverse to pass the information back up the chain of command, until the status of the new marketing initiative finally gets back to the President.

Upon assuming a new leadership position, one of the first things I tell my management team is: "Don't be surprised when I go directly to someone who works for you to get information. I will give assignments top down (most of the time), but I will usually go to the source for information. I don't much care for the chain of command. This is just my style." Coming from an ex-military guy, this is usually quite a surprise to people.

There are several good reasons why I do this:

Speed. It doesn't take a rocket scientist to understand that a quick phone call or visit to the source is a faster way to get information than passing messages up and down the chain of command.

Accuracy. Think about the party game where one person whispers a story to the person next to him or her who repeats the story to the next person, then to the next, and so on. The last person repeats the story out loud so that all can hear, and then everyone gets a good laugh about how much the story differs from when it started. Passing information up and down an organization's chain of command can have the same effect. And just like in the party game, the more people the messages pass through, the more chance there will be for misinterpretation.

> A CEO was reviewing his company's expenses and noticed a $3 million charge for outside legal services. He asked the Chief Legal Counsel how this compared to last year. Four layers up and down in the organization later, the answer came back that this was $2 million higher than last year's budget for outside legal fees. "Budget," the CEO said. "I don't care about how this compares to our budget; I want to know how much we spent on legal fees last year versus how much we spent this year." Four layers up and down the organization later, another answer came back that legal expenses for the current year were virtually equal to what had been spent last year. The wrong question somehow got communicated the first time up and down the chain of command – something that could have been avoided if the CEO had simply gone to the source.

No Filters. Direct feedback doesn't allow middle managers to put a "spin on a story." These filters have been attributed to the biggest reason for the downfall of John Akers at IBM. Many have said that John didn't know what was really going on at IBM because of the multiple layers of management between him and the field – including the multiple administrative assistants that often distorted information so that no 'bad news' reached John's executive office. One IBM insider, who worked for IBM during the John Akers era, told me that one of the first things Lou Gerstner did when he took over was to eliminate organizational filters so that he knew what was really going on.

People Allowed to do Real Work. When intermediaries up and down the chain of command are not collecting and relaying information, they are able to spend time doing other things, more productive things.

In the 1980s there was a big push to "flatten organizations" by eliminating middle management jobs. Middle managers, the theory went, didn't really do much work – they spent most of their workday collecting and relaying information up and down the chain of command. Many middle manager positions were eliminated, but leaders who continue to use the chain of command to request and collect information, perpetuate the problem.

Lets Employees Know You Care. When a leader calls or visits an employee directly to ask about what they are doing, it 1) lets them know that the leader knows what they are working on; 2) it reinforces that what they are working on is important.

Provides a Communication Opportunity. As much as you might try, you don't always talk to all of your employees on a daily/ weekly basis. Going to them – the source – for information gives you a communication opportunity that you might otherwise not have. Seize this opportunity to talk about other things – company and department performance, yesterday's football game, a recent marriage, etc. – or just to provide a little more positive reinforcement.

This is also an excellent tool for getting to know up-and-coming talented individuals on a personal basis. There are many talented people in your organization that you, as a leader, may not get to work with on a daily basis.

Great leaders scrap the chain of command. They go directly to the source for information, thus improving the speed, quality and accuracy of the information they receive, and freeing up their intermediate managers to do real work. Great leaders go to the source for information so that their employees know they care about the work they do.

Chapter Thirty-three: Remain Calm

"One of the tests of leadership is the ability to recognize a problem before it becomes an emergency."
- Arnold Glasgow

"Keep cool and you command everybody."
- Louis de Saint-Just

Great leaders remain calm even when the world appears to be falling down all around them. Great leaders know that if they panic, others are likely to panic too. They understand that employees may do the wrong thing when they are hurried and frazzled. So when everyone else is in a panic, the best leaders remain calm.

Many great leaders come to mind. Consider Franklin D. Roosevelt's statement in his first inaugural address on March 4, 1933:

> My firm belief is that the only thing we have to fear is fear itself – nameless, unreasoning, unjustified terror which paralyzes needed efforts to convert retreat into advance.

Also consider Michael Jordan, unarguably *the* leader of the six-time World Championship Chicago Bulls basketball teams in the 1990s. He always wanted the ball and he always got the ball at the end of a close game – no matter how good or bad he was playing on that particular day. He was the go-to guy because he didn't panic, no matter how big the game or how much pressure others might be feeling.

When I was a young boy, my grandmother would go to the chicken coop every Sunday to kill a chicken for dinner. I watched her chase the chicken around the yard until she caught it. Then I watched her chop off its head (not something I enjoyed). Occasionally, a chicken would get loose after losing its head and begin running around the yard, literally headless.

At this point, the chicken was understandably panicked and it was a chaotic sight to see it running around, with absolutely no clue of where it was going. So the phrase, "running around like a chicken with its head cut off" became synonymous with someone who was panicked out of control. It is an unpleasant but accurate description of how some leaders behave under pressure.

I instinctively knew the importance of remaining calm from the beginning of my leadership career. This was reinforced in my very first leadership role as an Air Force officer. Several months into my assignment, the non-commissioned officers who worked for me scheduled a meeting and simply said, "What we like most about you, Lieutenant, is that you don't panic. You don't overreact." (A corollary lesson here is that some of the best feedback and advice a leader gets is from the people he or she leads.) I began to pay attention and was surprised at how many of my fellow officers did panic under pressure. I felt so good about this that I have made it one of the cornerstones of my professional leadership career. I try hard to always remain calm.

Remaining calm is not always easy for a leader. As leaders we are constantly under pressure. Deadlines must be met. Budgets must be managed. Customers demand more. Unpleasant surprises occur. And, even if you remain calm, those who you lead, as well as those you follow, can get frazzled.

When I was based in Alaska, I returned from lunch one day to the sounds of the men and women in my organization singing:

From the halls of Montezuma; to the shores of Tripoli;
We fight our country's battles; on the land as on the sea

Then they began to laugh, hysterically.

They were singing the Marine Corps hymn. It turned out that in the short hour that I had been away, the personnel center had called to tell me that I (an Air Force officer) had been selected to attend a prestigious joint military school at the Marine Corps base in Quantico, Virginia. Hanging out with the Marines was something I was definitely not interested in – and the men and women in my unit knew this. They were, as the British say, attempting to "wind me up." They expected me to react – they expected me to panic.

But I didn't. Instead, I calmly called the personnel center and explained that if I had wanted to get shot at, I'd have joined the Marines. I asked them to find me another "prestigious" assignment. I was fortunate that a General Officer was looking after my career at this point, and I pretty much called the shots on what assignments I would and would not accept. So the personnel center found someone else to go to Quantico, Virginia, and I was given another assignment, more to my liking.

Leaders can stop panic by anticipating organizational anxiety and taking steps to avoid it. Consider the following example:

One of the most emotional things that can happen to employees is for a company to change their health benefits. In this day of rising health costs, many companies are lowering their benefits and/or raising the cost of healthcare to employees.

In one of my jobs the decision was made to change health care insurance companies. I knew employees would panic about this. I knew the questions they would ask. How much will this cost? Will my personal doctor – the one I have been seeing for years – the one who knows my health better than anyone else – be covered in the new plan? How will I file claims? Will the new plan be more cumbersome?

I talked with our Human Resource staff to get answers to these predictable questions. They assured me that the cost would be the same with the new insurance company. They told me it was very likely that my doctor would be in the new plan – if I wanted to verify this, I could log onto the new insurance provider's web site and check their physician listing. They let me know that claims would be just as easy to file and the process for seeking treatment would not change. In other words, the only thing that was changing was the name of the insurance company.

I told my staff of the pending change, and, at the same time, I reviewed the list of questions and answers I had gathered in advance. They didn't panic.

Other leaders, who hadn't anticipated the inevitable questions, didn't fare so well. The difference was that I had done my research and was able to pass on some reassuring words that immediately calmed things down.

Let me give you one final example from my work in the women's fashion retail industry. Women's fashion retail is a fast paced and information dependent business. It is important to know when merchandise is selling and when merchandise is not selling. It is important to know where sales are good and where sales are bad.

So, as the computer guy, one of the most important services I could provide was to process the hundreds of thousands of sales that occurred each week and report the results to our management team. Every Monday morning, the computers would spew out reams and reams of paper reports. The business depended on it. But, occasionally the computer would break and the reports would be late. That's when people began to panic, primarily because they knew the CEO was about to panic. It was not a pretty sight.

One of the guys who worked with me put it like this:

> When we worked together and people would panic
> when their Monday morning reports were an hour late,
> I would remind them that 'it was just girl clothes.' The

point being that even though it seemed like the end of the world if the President of the company didn't get his reports at 7:30 a.m. on Monday morning it really wasn't. Nobody was going to die because the reports were late. And honestly nobody was going to get fired either. The CEO may rant and rave but that shouldn't create panic. That's between him and his cardiologist.

Great leaders remain calm under pressure. They remain steady even when those they work with are frantic. Great leaders anticipate organizational anxiety and address employee issues and concerns up front, cutting panic off at the pass.

Chapter Thirty-four: Don't Get Cute with Organization Structure

"Any sufficiently advanced bureaucratic organization is indistinguishable from molasses."
- Unknown

When it comes to organization structure your mantra should be to *keep it simple*. Apply the following litmus test: Is your structure so complicated that your employees, customers, and/or suppliers don't understand it? If so it is probably too complicated.

When I worked for British Petroleum (BP) in the early 1980s, it was a huge multinational company with a complicated organization structure. Everyone at BP had at least three bosses. For instance, if you worked in the finance department in BP France, supporting the oil refining business, you reported to the Vice President of Finance (a functional boss), the President of BP France (a geographic boss), and the Vice President of Refining (a line of business boss). We called this the BP Matrix.

This organization confused everyone. One day, during an employee meeting, someone asked the Chairman if he could explain the BP Matrix. Proudly, he said:

It's like your family. If your son or daughter asks if they can borrow the car, what do you say? In my family, I tell them it's OK with me, but they should check with their mother. Their mother asks if they have checked with me, then says that it's OK with her, but check with your brother and sister to make sure they don't have something planned.

The BP Matrix works just like this. If you want to do something you should check with the president of your country organization, your line of business executive, and your functional executive. You may proceed if they all agree.

So under the BP Matrix organization structure, three different people had to say yes before an employee could do anything. That rarely happened, so not much got done. Many people in the organization could say no, but few could take brave, bold steps to say yes.

In the 1990s "teams" were all the rage. If you worked at a company that believed in teams, you could literally work for several different leaders on the same day, depending on which "teams" you had been assigned to. Or, worse yet, you could be assigned to a "self-directed" team – a team with no leader. Believe it or not there was a time when people thought this was a good idea. Thankfully, most came to realize that a team without a leader is like a ship with no rudder. Teams, like other organization structures, need leaders – someone to direct activities and make the occasional decision. When I form a team, I always make sure that the team has agreed on a leader. If not, I appoint one.

Organizations should be structured so that most employees have one, and only one, boss. Every employee has the right to know who this one person is. It is great to assign employees to several "teams," and they should support their teams' objectives and leaders. But, that doesn't mean they have more than one boss. One person should write an employee's annual performance appraisal, conduct their annual performance review, and determine their salary and bonus. That one person is their one boss.

In my experience, the best organization structures are clear, logical, non-bureaucratic, and business-aligned. Allow me to explain.

Clear. Your organization should be completely clear – there should be no ambiguity. Employees should be able to answer the question, "Who is your boss?" without hesitation. Customers should be able to figure out where to go for assistance. Suppliers should be able to figure out with whom they are doing business. Shareholders should know who is in charge.

Logical. Functions should be done where it makes the most sense. I inherited a headquarters group of people whose job was to represent field operations. These people had never worked in the field. They had never visited the field. Some of them had never worked in our industry segment prior to coming to work for us. This seemed illogical to me. So I asked the obvious question: Why isn't the field representing itself? Having not received a good answer, I restructured the organization so that the field represented the field.

Non-Bureaucratic. Good organization structures facilitate the process of getting things done. Bureaucratic organizations slow things down in committees and/or multiple approval processes, so that it is difficult to get things done.

One sign that you might be dealing with a bureaucratic organization is that you are encountering more roadblocks to keep work from being done, than ways to get things done.

My favorite example of a bureaucratic organization is the Ohio Department of Motor Vehicles. When I lived in Ohio, the DMV did their best to prevent you from registering your vehicle. Do you have cash or a money order? Do you have an emissions inspection? Do you have police validation that the Vehicle Identification Number (VIN) on your car or truck matches that on your vehicle registration? Do you have a signed power of attorney? Is it notarized? Etc., etc, etc. I couldn't help but think that this was backward. Shouldn't their objective have been to help you to get your vehicle registered?

Business-Aligned. The best way to structure your organization is to mirror the overall business organization. If your business is organized by geography, your organization should be also. If your business is organized by line of business, your structure should be aligned with that. If your business is structured along functional lines, so should you.

Let me give you an example. When I assumed my leadership position at one retailer, I discovered that the business was organized along the functional lines as follows: Merchandise, Distribution, Inventory Management, Finance, Human Resources, Real Estate, and Store Operations. My organization, the information technology organization, on the other hand, was organized around the technology we supported as follows: Computer Operations, Personal Computers & Networks, Unix Applications, and IBM Applications. Our internal customers needed a scorecard to figure out where to go for help. I immediately changed our organization to match the business. In the end, there was one person in my organization that managed the information technology support for each business function – regardless of the technology being used.

So don't get cute with organization structure. Keep it simple. Clear, logical, non-bureaucratic, business-aligned organizations work best. Most employees should have one and only one boss, so avoid multiple, conflicting reporting relationships. It's great to assign employees to teams, committees, or workgroups, but don't confuse these with reporting relationships. And when you form a team, make sure it has a leader.

Chapter Thirty-five: Hit the Road

"Santa Claus had the right idea. Visit everyone once a year."
- Victor Borges

It is very important for leaders to be visible. It is important for leaders to communicate directly with their constituents. Every time I visit a customer, a supplier, a field office, a store, a distribution facility, etc., I learn something valuable about my business. And, I develop new personal relationships. The importance of personal relationships with your key suppliers should never be underestimated. There will be a day when you will need something from your key suppliers, and if you have a personal relationship your objectives will be much easier to manage.

I have worked in a number of headquarters organizations. I have found that one of the best things a leader from headquarters can do is to hit the road and visit the field. Field employees tell me they appreciate my visits. They tell me how infrequently they see other leaders on their turf. They make sure I feel welcomed and appreciated because they want me to come back. Every time I visit the field I send a clear message that what they do is important and valued – and it is.

Let me give you a couple of examples:

1. The CEO at one retailer where I worked required corporate officers and buyers work in one of our stores every month. Yes, we were all required to get out of our chairs at headquarters and get our fingernails dirty. There were two rules. We all had to work in our stores on the same two days – to make sure we had similar customer, merchandise, and sales promotion experiences. And, we were

required to work in the same store, month after month, so we could develop a working relationship with the store's employees and get to know that store's customers.

This was a great program! It was expensive for all of us to travel to a store every month. But believe me, it paid big dividends.

I looked forward to my store workdays. I assisted and talked with customers. I stocked merchandise. I changed pricing and promotion materials. I spent quality time talking to our store employees. As a result, I always learned something valuable about our business.

One February, after a particularly disappointing holiday season, we were badly overstocked with merchandise. We had tried marking things down and had reached the point where we had priced items well below our costs – just to move them out of the store. But the customer still wasn't buying. All of us sitting at headquarters were puzzled and wondered why the merchandise wouldn't sell, even at these greatly reduced prices.

I discovered the problem in the first five minutes in the store by talking to our first customer of the day. I directed her to the sale racks. She looked at the $29.00 price tag, and to my surprise, asked what the original price had been. I looked at the price tag expecting to read the original price, and discovered it had been plastered over by a big red sticker. The customer couldn't see what a bargain they were being offered, because they could no longer see the original price. There was no way to tell how much the item had been marked down.

This was not our normal way of marking down merchandise. Typically, the original price was lined out with a red pen and the new, reduced price was hand-written above it. Placing a reduced price sticker over the original price violated one of the principle rules of retail sales – always make sure the customer knows the deal.

Upon further investigation, I discovered that someone in store operations had made an "efficiency" decision to equip the stores with price sticker machines. They figured it would be faster and cheaper for store employees to sticker the reduced price than to hand mark each item with a red pen. The stickers were so large that it was virtually impossible to apply them without blocking the original price. As soon as the stickers were removed, and the customer could clearly see both the discounted price and the original price, our over stocked merchandise began to sell.

2. At British Petroleum, the senior information technology leaders visited our strategic technology suppliers annually to 1) communicate our business strategies and directions; and 2) hear, firsthand, what new technology developments were coming. There were six of us in total. We commandeered the corporate jet and began our journey by stopping first in New York, where we visited Bell Laboratories. This was a hotbed of new technology development – after all this is where the transistor, the silicon chip, and fiber optic communications were developed. We then visited IBM's corporate offices and laboratory. The next stop was Digital Equipment Corporation before we headed to the West Coast and Apple Computer. It was a grueling four days, but the relationships we developed and the knowledge we gained made it very worthwhile.

I began this chapter by saying how important it is for leaders to be visible. Let's look at a leader that was invisible, and the consequences of that.

A person from outside the organization replaced the CFO. The new executive arrived at work early each morning, parked his car in an executive-only parking area in the basement of the building, and rode a private executive elevator nonstop, directly to the top floor executive suites.

He spent 16 hours each day in his office, after which he descended the executive elevator back to his executive parking spot and left for home. The only people who knew him, personally, were those whom he summoned to his office. No one else ever saw him.

The CFO was a powerful man. He was a change agent who began to drive significant change in the organization. His head and shoulders photo appeared in the company's magazine nearly every month, along with an article about the magnificent impact he was having on the company.

About six months after the CFO's arrival, my staff informed me that they had never seen him, physically, let alone met him. They wondered if he felt he was too good for the rest of us. I approached the CFO and suggested that he do a little walking around. Just so people could see and meet him.

What I didn't realize was that, in the absence of fact, people will imagine what a person is like. Because of his tremendous impact and his bold changes, everyone assumed the CFO was six foot four inches tall and weighed more than two hundred pounds. When he finally got out of his office, people were amazed that he was actually only four feet, eleven inches tall and weighed only about 120 pounds.

Everyone was astounded. They couldn't help but feel differently about him. After all, in their mind, they had visualized him as a giant. It would have been better had the CFO been more visible from the beginning.

So be visible. Hit the road. Don't make people come to you. Tell them what you are trying to do for them and ask for advice on how you can do even better. You will be surprised what you will learn about your business. And, there's nothing quite like good old face-to-face contact to build strong personal relationships.

Chapter Thirty-six:
Encourage People to Bring You Solutions – Not Problems

"Focus 90% of your time on solutions and only 10% of your time on problems."
- Anthony J. D'Angelo, *The College Blue Book*

"Within the problem lies the solution."
- Milton Katselas

Psychologists say that their patients usually come to them with the solution to their problem in mind. The trick is getting them to verbalize it. I believe that most employees also have a solution in mind when they bring problems to their leader.

Great leaders don't want employees to bring them only problems – they expect and encourage employees to also propose solutions. I learned this early on. I was working for an analytical-type Chief Information Officer (head computer geek) and he asked me to prepare a presentation for the CEO. He specifically told me to present several options.

"The CEO will want options," he said. "Give him at least three and be sure to outline the pros and cons of each. Don't give him a recommended solution. He will want to make the decision, himself."

That is exactly what I did. At the end of my presentation, the CEO (like any good leader) simply said. "What do *you* recommend?" It wasn't that he was uncomfortable making the decision. It certainly wasn't that he didn't understand the options. He genuinely wanted to know what I thought. He had hired me because I knew more about my function than he wanted or needed to know. He realized that I was better informed about what should be done than he was. I recommended option two and he concurred.

In most cases your job, as a leader, should be to endorse and support the recommendations of the good people in your organization. I want to know that we have options, but I also want my employees to tell me what they would do. I believe good leaders hire good people who are capable of making decisions and making sound recommendations. Let them do their job. As one of my former employees said:

> I remember you once said, 'If I have to make every decision for Kate (a director who reported directly to me) why do I need her?' It's a point that stuck with me. You shouldn't pay people to be Vice Presidents, Directors and Managers for them to complain about their problems and expect you, their boss, to make every decision.

So how do you encourage your employees to bring you solutions when they may be in the habit of only bringing you problems?

Ask the question: "What do you recommend?" When someone brings you a problem and doesn't offer a solution, simply ask for his or her recommended course of action – just like my CEO did to me. Most employees will have an opinion and they only need to be asked to offer it. Most will figure out that this is the way you like to operate and will start bringing you solutions along with their problems.

Agree with their recommendations more often than not. Do I always agree with my employees' recommendations? No. But, I agree most of the time, because most of the time, the people who come to me offer solid, logical solutions. The more you agree the more confidence your employees will have to keep bringing you solutions.

Remember that there is always more than one way to solve a problem. If the solution proposed is not the one you had in mind, ask yourself if it isn't just as good – just as likely to work – as your solution.

It is frustrating to offer advice and be ignored. Let me give you a personal example.

When I was working on my graduate degree at the University of Colorado, my wife and I lived next door to Suzie-Q, a widow who had lost her husband in a B-52 aircraft accident in the Air Force. She was left to raise their two young children on her own.

Suzie-Q asked for a lot of advice – but she rarely took it. I recall the following incident:

> Suzie-Q: "I have decided to buy myself a new refrigerator for Christmas this year, but I don't know what to buy. Should I get one with the freezer on top, a side-by-side, or one with the freezer on the bottom?"
>
> Me: "I don't know much about refrigerators, but I think my wife, Sharon, prefers a side-by-side. We had a refrigerator with the freezer on the bottom once, and I know she definitely didn't care for that."
>
> Suzie-Q: "What brand would you recommend?"
>
> Me: "I really don't know. You might try calling Frank. He might have an opinion."
>
> Suzie-Q: "I'd really appreciate it if you would give me some advice on this. I don't know anything about refrigerators."
>
> Me: "OK. I knew an appliance repairman once who said to stay away from General Electric."

> *Three weeks later:*

Suzie-Q: "Guess what? I just bought a new refrigerator."

Me: "That's great. What did you buy?"

Suzie-Q: "A General Electric with the freezer on the bottom."

Suzie-Q asked for my advice, and then she did the exact opposite of what I had recommended. Knowing Suzie-Q she had probably asked advice from a dozen other people, and maybe she took their recommendation. But she didn't take mine. This sort of thing happened all the time. Just think about how frustrating this type of thing can be in the workplace.

Recognize those who bring you solutions. In your next staff meeting or department meeting, make a big deal about how John not only identified a problem but also pinpointed a great solution. This type of public praise will stimulate not only John to bring you more solutions, but it sends the message to others that you appreciate employees who bring you solutions.

Part of the reason I encourage employees to offer solutions to problems is selfish. I make a hundred decisions every week. If I tried to make *all* the decisions, there wouldn't be enough time. It just makes sense for me to encourage my employees to bring me solutions – not just problems. That way I can work more reasonable hours.

Great leaders, the ones who have hired the very best people, should have the savvy and intelligence to allow their employees to make recommendations and propose solutions. Encourage them to do it. In fact, insist that they do it. To not do so is arrogant. It implies that only you, the leader, can solve problems. You don't always have to agree with their solutions, but, if you have hired the very best people, I predict you will agree most of the time.

Chapter Thirty-seven:
Be Careful What You Say

"It takes tremendous discipline to control the influence, the power you have over other people's lives."
- Clint Eastwood

I was in the General's office one day with some of his higher ranking staff. The meeting had gone on for nearly an hour, and the General got up from his chair to stretch his legs. He stepped up to his office window, gazed out onto the landscape and casually remarked, "I never really noticed that fire hydrant down there near the parade ground before. It's kind of a strange place for a fire hydrant."

Then he shrugged his shoulders and returned to his chair to resume the discussions.

The chief civil engineer immediately asked to be excused to make an urgent phone call. Within a half an hour, we heard a ruckus outside the office. We all went to the window where we saw a six-man crew frantically working to relocate the fire hydrant. The General never intended for his off the cuff remark to result in such an extreme reaction.

There is a similar story about a financial tycoon who was playing at one of *his* golf courses (he owned two) when he noticed that some brickwork along a cart path was not – in his opinion – laid in a graceful enough arc. He complained about this rather loudly. Two hours later, the bricks had been ripped out and the stonemason was starting over. Even the financial tycoon was amazed at the power of his words.

Finally, I once worked in an organization where the chief

operating officer was convinced that people weren't working hard enough. So, he began to "take attendance." His office window overlooked the employee parking lot. Unbeknownst to employees, the chief operating officer showed up thirty minutes early each morning to watch people arriving for work. He dutifully recorded their time of arrival. Similarly, he began to watch for people leaving thirty minutes ahead of the workday's end – also marking those who left early. After several weeks of this, he called his staff together and made the following statement:

> I have been keeping track of our employees' comings and goings and it is clear to me that we are not getting a full day's work from some of them. There are employees who show up five to ten minutes late and there are other employees who leave five or ten minutes early.
>
> From this point forward, I want to make one thing clear. Our office hours are 8:00 a.m. to 5:00 p.m., Monday through Friday, with one hour for lunch. I expect everyone to be in his or her desks at 8:30 a.m. and no one should leave the office until 5:00 p.m. each day.

So that is what everyone did. The few employees, who had shaved five or ten minutes off the workday, quit doing that and showed up on time and left on time. They also took their full one-hour lunch break, whereas before the boss' edict to adhere to a strict work schedule, they only took a half-hour lunch break and went back to work early.

In addition, the majority of employees who had been showing up a half an hour early and/or leaving a half an hour late, also began to show up on time and leave on time. And those employees who had worked several hours a day at home and/or worked the occasional

Saturday or Sunday morning stopped doing that as well.

There are a million things wrong with the way this leader approached this problem. To start with, why should or would a senior executive spend an hour out of his workday, every day, for weeks, taking attendance? This doesn't seem very "leader like" to me. Second, he should not have generalized the faults of a few tardy and eager to leave individuals to the entire organization. It turned out that only a handful of employees were cutting the workday short. Why not deal with them and them alone. But, the biggest mistake the leader made was making a public statement that he expected everyone to be in his or her desks on time and to leave the office on time every day.

He had asked for everyone to work an eight-hour day, and that is exactly what he got. No one came late or left early. But no one worked overtime either. This leader and his organization would have been far better off demonstrating flexibility and a results oriented environment – not a "buns in seat" attendance policy.

It is also important that leaders are careful about how they say things. Tone of voice, facial expressions and eye contact (or lack thereof) both send messages.

Even the way in which you present a list can be important. Let's say that you want to list ten important things for your organization to work on. Others immediately assume that the first item listed is the most important. And, if you number the items 1-10 this notion is only reinforced. Surely the item number one must be the most important? The same is true when listing people – if there is no other pattern identifiable, others will assume that the person you list first is the most important. One of the great leaders I worked for at British Petroleum taught me how to deal with this propensity of people assuming the first thing or person listed is the most important:

> When listing people – do so alphabetically. That way the person whose name begins with 'A' will not get the false impression that he is more important than

the person whose name begins with 'Z'

When listing other things use bullets instead of numbers, and always emphasize that the list is in no particular order – unless you want the list to be prioritized in which case use numbers.

What a leader says and how he or she says it can be very powerful. As a leader, be careful what you say – as the stories above illustrate someone may take you literally and do exactly what you say.

Chapter Thirty-eight: Minimize Rumors

"A lie can travel halfway around the world while the truth is putting on its shoes."
- Mark Twain

"A rumor without a leg to stand on will get around some other way."
- John Tudor

I would like to have titled this chapter *Eliminate* Rumors (as opposed to *Minimize* Rumors). But I've learned that, in spite of all my best efforts, I can't eliminate rumors – the best I can do is to hold them to a minimum. Given their potential harm, the fewer rumors floating around, the better.

In my opinion rumors are cancer to an organization. Why are rumors so harmful? First, rumors consume time and energy – time and energy employees could otherwise spend doing productive work. Second, even though rumors are usually partially true they also usually contain a good deal of incorrect information. Spreading rumors propagates incorrect information. As the rumor spreads people will hear the same rumor from multiple sources, adding credence to it. If employees believe the falsehoods they may head in the wrong direction.

I recently saw, first hand, how a rumor adversely affected an organization. I invited one of our strategic business partners to a meeting to resolve an important issue in one of our business units. On the plane ride, the account executive told me, "The rumor is that our company will announce major organization changes today." Once we arrived, our strategic business partners were on their cell phones asking others back home if there was any news to report. As the day progressed it appeared they were only partially present for our meeting. They were physically at our meeting but mentally they were focused on the rumored organization change. They checked their messages at every break. They scanned the Internet from their laptops. For this day, they were preoccupied with a rumor.

Finally, late in the day, word came that indeed there had been an organization change. It was not a *major* change as had been rumored, but a much less significant change. It was no big deal.

This illustrates two characteristics of rumors. First, the rumor was only partially true, having been magnified as it was repeated and spread throughout the organization. Instead of the major change that had been rumored, only a minor organization change occurred. It also illustrates how consumed people can become with rumors. These people had become so consumed they let it affect their contribution to the day's important work.

Why do rumors exist? Some of it is human nature. People like to gossip about other people – some more than others. But the main reason rumors exist is to fill a factual information void. Rumors start to fill a communication gap. In the absence of fact, employees will make things up and rumors will take over.

The following are some things I do to minimize rumors:

Tell Employees What's Going On. The best way to stop rumors – before they even start – is to tell employees what's really going on. Give them all the facts – don't lie. If there is something you can't tell them (something that is personal or confidential) let them know the reason. You should be able to tell employees almost everything. As long as you are communicating, employees will have less need to "make things up." As they learn that your style is to be honest and candid with them, they will be more likely to dismiss unfounded rumors, as their normal course of action.

Keep Employees Busy. Rumors are more likely to spread when employees have idle time on their hands. People who are busy and challenged have less time and energy to devote to the rumor mill. I first noticed this when I led the Information Services organization at British Petroleum America. The company was cutting back – downsizing – and employees knew their jobs could be at risk. Those employees who weren't busy spent more time on scuttlebutt than those who had their hands full with meaningful work did.

Don't React. As a leader, the worst thing you can do is to react to rumors. I worked for one CEO who reacted to every rumor he heard. He enjoyed walking up and down the halls and engaging people in conversation – this is a good thing. Unfortunately, he also thrived on rumors. He encouraged rumors. One day, during the course of a hallway conversation, someone said, "I don't know this for a fact, but I've heard a rumor that Rob is using company computers and time to play fantasy football." The CEO immediately went on a witch-hunt to find out if Rob was indeed playing fantasy football on company time (it turned out he wasn't). But, the CEO had sent the message that he was interested in rumors, and that he wanted to hear about rumors. My advice is that when someone brings you a rumor you send the opposite message. Tell them you deal in facts – not rumor – and that you recommend they do the same.

Head Them Off At The Pass. Sometimes a rumor will get started in spite of your best efforts to communicate what's going on and your best efforts to make sure employees know the facts. When this happens, stop it quickly by filling the information void. I stick with the principle outlined above – don't react. But, at the first opportunity, set the facts straight.

For example, I once heard a rumor that my manager, the Chief Financial Officer of the company, was about to be fired. I knew this was false. In fact, the truth was he was about to be promoted to a newly created Chief Operating Officer position with even more responsibility. We wanted to keep this confidential so we didn't want our investors and financial analysts to hear about such a significant change from anyone but us.

I knew that this was the type of rumor that would spread like wildfire. I used my morning staff meeting to squelch the rumor before it could get started. I simply said, "I have heard the rumor that my manager is about to be fired. This is absolutely false, and you should tell that to anyone you hear spreading this falsehood. There are some changes contemplated at our executive level, but they are all positive. I'm sorry, but I must keep these details confidential, but there will be an announcement day after tomorrow, and I think you will all be pleased. I will let you know more when it's appropriate."

Give Direct Answers to Direct Questions. When someone asks you a question, give him or her a direct answer. People sense when their leader is being evasive and they assume you are hiding something. This fuels speculation – the root of all rumors.

Be Prepared to Tell Employees It's None of Their Business. There are some things that are just nobody's business. Suppose Jim tells you he has been diagnosed with terminal cancer and he's asked you to keep it confidential. Suppose Helen has confided that she and her husband are getting a divorce. If someone asks you about situations like these, politely tell them you're pretty sure that it is none of their business.

Rumors are like cancer to an organization. They occupy time and energy that would otherwise be available to do productive work, and they potentially lead employees to make decisions and take actions based on incorrect information.

Great leaders understand they can't eliminate rumors, but they also know they can keep them to a minimum. Tell employees what's going on so they don't have to fabricate rumors. Encourage employees to come to you if they have questions and make your answers direct and honest. Don't react to rumors – tell people you deal only in facts and that you suggest they do the same. When, in spite of all your efforts to the contrary, a rumor begins to spread, head it off at the pass. The longer a rumor is allowed to propagate, the more credence it obtains.

Chapter Thirty-nine:
Know When to Fall on Your Sword

"Fall seven times, stand up eight."
- Japanese Proverb

"If one sticks too rigidly to one's principles, one would hardly see anybody."
- Agatha Christie

I admire people who stand by their principles. I respect people who take a position and stick with it. But, great leaders know that not all issues are worth going to battle over. Great leaders know when to fall on their sword. And, great leaders know when to stop discussing something and just get on with it. Let me give you a few examples.

My first experience with this came as a young manager at British Petroleum America. Voice mail was just arriving on the scene as a brand new technology. We still had literally hundreds of tape answering machines connected to office telephones around our headquarters building when we brought the first voice mail system into the offices. The answering machines disappeared and people became so much more productive. This was several years before electronic mail came on the scene, and much of what we now use electronic mail for was being done with voice mail in these early days. The key catch phrase was "non-synchronous communication," meaning that you could literally carry on a two-way conversation with someone by leaving asynchronous messages back and forth – without ever talking directly to him or her.

Soon our corporate executives were singing the praises of voice mail and our field offices began to request the same service. I put my enterprise-wide hat on and concluded that we would all be even more productive if we adopted the same brand of system and networked them together. We had already stopped playing telephone tag with each other at the headquarters. It would be great if we could forward, reply, and send voice messages in the same way to the entire company. I discussed this with our affiliate IT Managers and everyone agreed except for one. For some reason, the IT manager in Houston liked a different brand. And, Houston was one of our largest field offices.

This really got my dander up. Everyone else could see the benefits of networking the same brand of voice mail systems together, all across the company. Why couldn't he see it? I began to complain loudly about him wanting to be different.

That's when my manager came to me and simply said, "Les, this one isn't worth falling on your sword over." And he was right. It didn't occur to me to back off until he said it. It wasn't my nature to back off. But after listening to my manager, I realized that everyone else in our business would be enjoying the benefits of networked voice mail systems. It was Houston's loss – not mine. Eventually he realized he was the odd man out and he came around. I didn't have to fall on my sword to make this happen.

On another occasion, one of the young men who worked for me called one day to tell me he had great news and not so great news. He joyfully told me that his wife had delivered their first child the night before – a healthy baby boy. The not so great news was that the hospital was discharging his wife and his new son that day – less than 24 hours after the baby had been born. In fact, they were packing as we spoke. The reason for the fast discharge was that our company's health plan only paid for one overnight stay. I couldn't believe it.

This was something worth falling on my sword over. I marched down to our benefits department and was told that yes, this was our policy. I asked if this wasn't a bit unreasonable. They told me it was not. They said that recent studies had found that it was good for the new mother and baby to get home soon – the sooner the better. My next stop was the Vice President of Human Resources, who gave me the same answer. My final stop was the CEO. She, like me, couldn't believe we were doing this. Shortly thereafter, our health insurance policy was changed. I spoke with that new father a few months ago and he commented on this incident.

> I remember when my first child Joseph was born and we had to leave the hospital after less than 24 hours. That was the medical rule at the time. Even though the issue was really over and you could have just let it go you took the issue up the ladder and made a lot of noise about it. As a result, the rule was changed and benefited others to follow – including my second and third child.

Let me give you another story about falling on your sword. I was a young Air Force officer stationed in Alaska. The winters were long and hard. It snowed by Halloween every year. It continued to snow all winter long and none of it melted until May. Temperatures reached negative 35 degrees Fahrenheit. In the middle of December, we had 20 hours of darkness per day. Many of our military men and women suffered from what was termed "cabin fever." They felt confined and trapped by the cold temperatures, large quantities of snow, and the long, dark days of winter.

So when summer finally arrived in June, everyone was anxious to get out and about. They went fishing, hunting, camping, sight seeing – anything to get out of the house, off the military base, and to be active. Every weekend there was a mass exodus from the Air Force base. More than half the people on the base left. For the most part, everyone understood the need for our military men and women to escape from the place where they had been trapped for eight or nine months.

One day, the commanding officer, General Bailey, began to worry about this. He worried that, with so many people away on weekends, we would be vulnerable to an attack. We were not at war, unless you call the Cold War a war. This was 25 years prior to 9/11/ 01. There was no reason to believe we would be attacked. When we heard of the General's concern, we began to joke that he was afraid that the Russians would decide to ice skate across the Bearing Strait some weekend and our military base would be vulnerable because so many people were outdoors enjoying their short summer season.

But this was no joke to the General. He issued a dictate that only one-fourth of all military personnel would be allowed to be away from the base on any given weekend. He instituted an elaborate scheme to make sure that this dictate was followed. Every weekend 75% of all military men and women were confined to the base, waiting for an attack that no one, except the General, believed would ever occur.

Six weeks later, at the General's weekly staff meeting, his senior officers were giving their reports. When it came to the chief medical officer, the dialogue went something like this:

> Chief Medical Officer: "General, there has been a sharp increase in the number of people seeking medical attention for psychiatric problems. There is a lot of summer 'cabin fever' going on."
>
> General: "Colonel. To what do you attribute this?"
>
> Chief Medical Officer: "General, our men and women need their weekend summer getaways. Your decision to take that away from them is taking its toll."

The chief medical officer decided this was an issue worth falling on his sword over. He challenged the General's confinement policy. He should have done this in private – challenging the commanding officer's policies in public was a sure way to get fired – which he did. But the General reversed his policy.

Successful leaders have strong principles and stand by them.

They aren't afraid to challenge policies and decisions. But great leaders understand that once a decision is made, it is time to get on board, support it, and move forward. The mantra should be to either get on board or find somewhere else to work.

I was the Chief Information Officer for a prominent retailer for four years. The first three years the company was decentralized and every operating division had its own Information Technology organization. During the fourth year, we made the decision to centralize all support functions. The Information Technology organization, just like Human Resources, Marketing, Planning, and all other support functions began to reduce in size and scope within the operating divisions and expand in size and scope in the corporate offices. I wasn't terribly excited about the change. The company had succeeded in the past due in large part to each operating division functioning, as its own independent, entrepreneurial entity with little or no interference from the corporate office.

We recruited a person from outside the company to be our new corporate Chief Information Officer (CIO) – the person who would eventually be my boss. The person we hired had strong credentials – on paper. But shortly after he arrived, we learned that our new CIO was not all he had presented himself to be. During the interview process he told us he was on the Board of Directors for the IBM Corporation. This was pretty impressive except that IBM didn't know who he was. He also bragged about attending Stanford University. It turned out that he only attended Stanford for one semester. He then transferred to a junior college and didn't graduate. Next, his resume said he had been the CIO for a major U.S. company. Turns out he was the deputy CIO – close but no cigar. Every time we turned over another rock we discovered an untruth. The list began to grow by leaps and bounds.

In the end, I could get behind the decision to centralize the information technology function, but I couldn't respect a person who stretched the truth to the extent that our new CIO had done. I knew I had only two choices. I could either fake my respect for someone or I could leave the company. I left the company.

Some corporate cultures are more open to debate and discussion than other corporate cultures. You, the leader, and your organization need to be in line with that. If your organization is pro-debate and discussion, you need to provide a forum for this to occur prior to implementing new processes. If your company is not pro-debate, you need to listen to objections, but be prepared to move swiftly to action. In either case, there is a point at which debate and discussion have to stop and things need to move forward.

There are a variety of ways to voice your concerns and stand by your principles. One good way to present your opposing view is to preface it by saying, "Let me play devil's advocate."

Successful leaders have strong principles and stand by them. But, successful leaders also understand that not every issue is worth battling. Great leaders encourage and participate in lively debates over key decisions. But once a decision is made, great leaders get behind it and help make it happen. Those who can't do this should go elsewhere.

Chapter Forty: Jack J. Woods – My First Leadership Challenge

"Some of the toughest leadership challenges are the managerial equivalent of herding cats."
- Unknown

I didn't have to wait long for my first leadership challenge. I met him on my first day on the job as a Second Lieutenant in the United States Air Force. His name was Jack J. Woods. I won't ever forget Jack J. Woods and the many challenges he gave me.

Jack was an 18-year Air Force veteran who had managed to reach the lowly position of Staff Sergeant – the minimum rank he could have achieved without being involuntarily separated from military service. I met Jack my first day on the job.

Here's how our first meeting went.

> First Sergeant: "Lieutenant Duncan, I'd like you to meet Staff Sergeant Woods, one of your shift supervisors."
>
> Me: "Nice to meet you Sergeant Woods."
>
> Jack J. Woods: "Yes sir, it's very nice to meet you too. We have been looking forward to your arrival. We've heard some very good things about you."
>
> Me: "Thank you Sergeant Woods. It's great to be here, and I look forward to working with you."
>
> Jack J. Woods: "Sir, may I ask you where you attended College and what your degree is in?"

Me: "I attended college at Wichita State University and have a Bachelor of Science degree in mathematics."

Jack J. Woods: "You know, I am attending college right now also. I am studying to be a surgeon." (I was momentarily impressed.)

Me: "Wow, that's wonderful. Where are you going to medical school and how far along are you?"

Jack J. Woods: "I am taking one course per semester via correspondence school and I've only just begun. I hope to be finished by the time I retire in a few years." (I was suddenly less impressed.)

Me: "That is very interesting. You are the first person I've known to study to be a doctor via correspondence school."

Jack J. Woods: "There's something else I need to tell you Lieutenant."

Me: "OK, shoot."

Jack J. Woods: "I have three part time jobs in addition to my full time Air Force job. But I want to assure you that none of my part time jobs will interfere with my Air Force responsibilities. First, I sell Amway products. Second, I am a salesman for a home delivery food company. Finally, I occasionally work at Sears at the mall."

Me: "Sergeant Woods, you must understand that your first responsibility is to the Air Force. Even one part time job could interfere with that – and you have not one but three part time jobs. That does concern me."

Jack J. Woods: "Amway and the home food delivery jobs are both pyramid schemes. My main job is recruiting others who will sell for me and then I get a cut of everything they earn. So once I get a few men and women working for me, I won't have to actually do any work – I'll just sit back and collect the cash.

"As for my job at Sears, I set my own hours. You see, I was shopping in the garden tool section of the store a few weeks back, and I noticed another customer having trouble deciding which shovel he should buy. I told him I'd buy the Craftsman shovel because they were guaranteed for life. If anything ever happened to the Craftsman shovel he could bring it back and Sears would give him a brand new one.

"Well, the Vice President of Sales for all of Sears Roebuck and Company was in the store that day and heard my advice to this other customer. He walked up to me and said he'd like for me to work in his store.

"I tried to explain that I already had a full-time job in the Air Force and two part time jobs, and that I wasn't sure how much time I would have to work at Sears. He told me not to worry about that. He said that any time I felt like working a few hours I should just come in. If someone else was already there working they'd send them home. So, I could hardly refuse a deal like this."

So in a matter of a few minutes Jack J. Woods had told me that he was studying to be a surgeon via a correspondence school and that he had been offered a totally flexible working arrangement at the local Sears store by the company's Vice President of Sales. I may not be the brightest bulb on the tree, but I recognized immediately that Jack J. Woods was a professional liar.

This was the first of many times that Jack J. Woods fed me a line of nonsense. I learned quickly that the only way to deal with him was with punishment – negative reinforcement – something I don't believe in. But, in Jack's case it was the only thing that worked.

Jack was one of four shift supervisors under my command. Each of my supervisors had 7 people working for them and each of these teams worked rotating shifts. They worked two day shifts followed by two evening shifts and then two midnight shifts. So eight men and women were scheduled to be on duty every hour of every day. But, Jack's night shifts often consisted of only two people. Jack would just give himself and most others the night off – so they would have the energy to sell Amway or home food delivery or whatever.

The word got to me that this was going on so I made a surprise visit at 2:00 a.m. one night, and sure enough there were only two people on duty – and Jack wasn't one of them. The two who were working were overwhelmed and work was piling up high. The next shift would spend the first several hours just catching up for Jack's shift.

I confronted Jack. He had a million excuses. I told him there were no legitimate excuses for having only two people on duty and that the next time he pulled that he would be disciplined. After this, I began to receive regular middle of the night phone calls from Jack's men and women explaining that they had a family emergency or some other good reason for leaving work, and asking my permission. I learned later that this was a ploy – wake the Lieutenant up in the middle of the night and he will eventually tell us to go back to running our own business. It didn't work.

One night Airman Jones called at 2:30 a.m. "Lieutenant Duncan," he said. "I was working and a metal sliver has lodged itself into my eye and Sergeant Woods told me I needed to call you before I left to go to the hospital." I was furious. First I told him to leave for the hospital immediately and to hand the phone to Jack J. Woods. I calmly asked Sergeant Woods what he used for brains and then told him this was the last straw. I demanded he stay over from his midnight shift so that he and I could have a good talk. Jack was severely disciplined the next day.

There were many irresponsible incidents and I levied punishment each and every time. But I didn't kick him out of the service, because Jack kept promising me that he was going to retire in two years. With only one year left, the Air Force screwed up and promoted him. Don't ask me why – it's a long story. But suffice it to say that if it had been up to me, it wouldn't have happened. After his promotion, Jack approached me to tell me he was re-enlisting. "Over my dead body,"

I said. "You've been nothing but trouble and you have enough stuff on your record to be removed from service forcefully. Jack, you have two choices. You can retire peacefully next year as you promised or you can submit your re-enlistment papers. If you do the latter, I will not support you and I will pursue court martial to end your term of service." Jack decided to leave peacefully.

On his way out Jack hit me with two final amazing things.

He told me that his term of active duty had been extended for two months so that he could have some dental work done. He explained that it had been eight years since he'd seen a dentist and that his discharge physical examination had revealed some serious dental issues. I asked him how he could have gone eight years without seeing a dentist. The Air Force "ordered" men and women to undergo a dental examination every six months. Failing to comply with this order would have landed him in additional trouble. "Oh, that was easy," he said. "I would receive my order every six months and schedule an appointment. I discovered that this was all I *had* to do – make the appointment – they took me off the list. Then just a day or so before my scheduled time at the dentist, I'd call and cancel it, claiming that I was about to be sent on a critical assignment, didn't know when I would be back, and would have to call to reschedule at a later date. I just did this for eight years." Wow! What a lot of trouble to go through just to avoid seeing a dentist. Wouldn't it have been easier to just go to the dentist?

He asked for my help in getting a retiree sticker for his car – something that would allow him to come back on base to shop at the discounted commissary and base-exchange and use the base hospital facilities. Retirees were allowed these privileges. Jack explained that he had never really had a sticker on his car before and the base authorities were reluctant to give him one now. Hesitantly, I asked why/how Jack had not had an active duty sticker on his car? He would have needed a sticker just to get past the guards every day, right?

"Oh no," said Jack. "I got to know the guards pretty well and they would just wave me through."

"But, Jack, why wouldn't you have just gotten a sticker like everyone else?" I said.

"Without a sticker, I could park just about anywhere I wanted to and not get a ticket. I almost always parked in the General's place on night shifts, for example, and got away with it. The military police assumed I was a civilian visitor and just placed a caution note on my windshield. If I'd had a military sticker on my car, I could have been arrested."

I will always remember Jack J. Woods – my first leadership challenge. He tried to wear me down, but I wouldn't let him. He gave me nothing but trouble and I gave him nothing but trouble back.

Chapter Forty-one: Top Ten List

In Chapter Nine I talked about my top-ten list and said that I believed no one should try to focus on more than ten things simultaneously.

This book contains more than forty chapters, each of which addresses a characteristic or behavior that I've been told has made me a great leader. True to my word, the following are the top ten things I believe can help you be a great leader:

1. **Know Your Business**. Leaders should be more than a functional or technical specialist. Great leaders understand their business and industry better than anyone else does. Great leaders structure their department's goals and objectives to support business goals and objectives and to overcome industry challenges.

2. **Surround Yourself with the Very Best People**. Great leaders know they can be even better with the right supporting cast. Great leaders are not afraid to hire people as good as or better than they are. The best leaders make very few hiring mistakes and have low employee turnover.

3. **Provide Positive Reinforcement – Tons of It**. For most people, positive reinforcement works better than criticism. Praise employees for the good job they are doing. Do it publicly. Tell their family and friends how much you appreciate their work. Learn to overlook the occasional mistake. Focus on the positive.

4. **Communicate Effectively**. Employees always want more communication. The problem in most organizations is not a lack of communication – the problem is a lack of *effective communication*. Great leaders are great communicators.

5. **Communicate the Big Picture**. Employees are more

productive when they see how their daily work fits into the broader business scheme. Consider doing a top ten list to keep people focused on what's truly important.

6. **Be Egalitarian**. Adopt the philosophy of working *with* employees. Employees already know they work for you – knowing that you are also working with them to achieve common goals and objectives will make your organization stronger.

7. **Have the Courage to Make Tough Decisions**. This is why leaders are paid the big bucks. Truly great leaders have the courage to make tough calls and to stand by them. When in doubt, do the right thing.

8. **Manage Your Time Effectively**. Time is something we all want more of. Great leaders don't work 60 hours a week. Great leaders don't work weekends. Great leaders manage their time effectively.

9. **Develop Excellent Relationships with Strategic Business Partners.** You probably deal with dozens of vendors and suppliers. Pick those who are strategic – those who can help your business best meet its goals and objectives – and treat them like true business partners. Look for win-win situations.

10. **Hit the Road.** It is important for leaders to be visible. It is important for leaders to communicate directly with their customers, business partners, field operations, plants, and factories. Hit the road and visit them. Don't make them come to you. Tell them what you are trying to do for them and ask for advice on how you can do even better.

Focus on these ten things and I believe you will be a more effective leader. Then take on a few more things and I am confident you will become a great leader.

Epilogue: Parallels Between Good Parenting and Good Leadership

"A child of five would understand this. Send someone to fetch a child of five."
- Groucho Marx

I asked a number of people to review the initial manuscript for this book and I received many constructive, helpful comments about how to make it better. One consistent message was – "I'd like to hear more about the similarities between being a good parent and being a good leader."

I have mentioned some of the parallels between parenting and leading along the way. I could write probably write an entire book about this. But, for the time, I will summarize my thoughts in the following paragraphs:

Learn from the Best and Worst. I have worked for many leaders in my life – some of them were excellent leaders and some were not so good. I learned how to become a great leader, in part, by imitating the behaviors of the really good leaders and avoiding the approaches of some of the not so good ones. Just as you can learn how to be a better leader from the actions of others, you can also be a better parent if you imitate the good things your parents did when they raised you, and avoid making the same mistakes they made.

Set High Expectations. Great leaders expect their employees to achieve more than they can. They set high expectations for them and aren't surprised when they achieve them. Great parents do the same with their children. When I was a child, my parents and grandparents expected me to become President of the United States or at least a

United States Senator. This was back in the dark ages when being President or a United States Senator was highly regarded. They expected me to go to college first – even though none of them were college educated. Their high expectations for me – and their confidence that I could achieve them – are part of the reason for my success today.

Praise a Lot. Great leaders are proud of their employees and praise them at every opportunity. They focus on the positive. The best parents raise their children in a positive environment of encouragement – they use punishment sparingly and never publicly humiliate their children.

Once, when I was nine years old, we visited the home of one of my father's co-workers. The family we visited had children the same age as me and my siblings. All the children were playing in the living room, when one started to make a little too much noise. His father jumped out of his chair, grabbed his son, took off his leather belt, pulled the boys pants down, and proceeded to repeatedly whip him until there were welts on his butt. I will never forget the negative impression that this very public, humiliating discipline had on me.

Set a Good Example. Great parents – like great leaders – understand that what they say and do has a profound influence over others. Do as I say, not as I do doesn't fly for leaders. It certainly doesn't fly when raising children either. The following lines from Dorothy Law Nolte are a powerful reminder of our influence:

If children live with criticism, they learn to condemn.
If children live with hostility, they learn to fight.
If children live with ridicule, they learn to be shy.
If children live with shame, they learn to feel guilty.
If children live with tolerance, they learn to be patient.

If children live with encouragement, they learn confidence.
If children live with praise, they learn to appreciate.

If children live with fairness, they learn justice.
If children live with security, they learn to have faith.
If children live with approval, they learn to like themselves.
If children live with acceptance and friendship, they learn to find love in the world.

Communicate. Great leaders are effective communicators. So are great parents. According to **parentssource.com**, only 26 percent of youth experience positive family communication. They advise parents to start talking with their children early – "Talk to young children every night before bed, and before you know it, your teenager will be knocking on your door for a goodnight chat."

Don't Fight Their Battles for Them. Great leaders teach their employees to resolve their own conflicts. The best parents teach their children the same. Like many parents, when my sons had disagreements, they came to their mother or me to referee. We rarely did. Instead, we encouraged them to work it out themselves. I believe this taught them a valuable life lesson. That they shouldn't look to others to solve their problems – they have to fight their own battles.

Take a Sincere Personal Interest. How many parents do you know that are not interested in their children? Probably not many. But how many parents do you know that are *sincerely* interested in their children – parents who put their children before everything else in their lives?

I am an avid golfer. Playing golf is one of the few burning passions in my life. A round of golf takes four to five hours to play – taking four to five hours out of a Saturday or Sunday just didn't feel right to me when I had three young boys. So I stopped playing when they were young. Instead, I coached their soccer teams. I attended their baseball games, their school concerts, recitals, plays, etc. I can count on one hand how many events I missed in my children's lives. I scheduled my work around my children's lives. I remember flying home, very late one weekday evening, just so I wouldn't miss my second son's fourth birthday. If my children didn't know then, I'm sure they know now that I did this because I was sincerely interested in them. The same principles apply to good leadership.

Be Present for the Moment. Today's fast-paced electronic society has many of us trying to do three or four things at the same time. We talk on our cell phones while we drive to work, while at the same time being preoccupied with the big meeting scheduled later in the day. Being fully present for each and every moment will improve relationships with co-workers and business associates. Focusing only on what they are saying lets them know that what they are telling you is important to you – their leader. Similarly, when your children feel heard and appreciated, they feel better about you, about themselves and about their family. Take the time to listen intensely to your children. Give them your full attention during those precious moments when you are together. As William Shakespeare said, "It is a wise father that knows his own child."

The greatest leaders I've known have also been great parents. In my opinion, this is no coincidence. The same skills and principles apply.

As I said at the beginning of this chapter, I could probably write an entire book about the parallels between good parenting and good leading. Allow me to close with a quote that my mother can probably identify with:

My mother had a great deal of trouble with me, but I think she enjoyed it.
- Mark Twain

Printed in the United States
25121LVS00002B/49

9 781413 731828